THE INFORMATION SOCIETY

A Study of Continuity and Change

Second Edition

JOHN FEATHER

Professor of Library and Information Studies and
Pro-Vice-Chancellor of Loughborough University

LIBRARY ASSOCIATION PUBLISHING
LONDON

© John Feather 1998

Published by
Library Association Publishing
7 Ridgmount Street
London WC1E 7AE

Library Association Publishing is wholly owned by The Library Association.

First published 1994
This second edition 1998

British Library Cataloguing in Publication Data

A catalogue record for this book is available from the British Library.

ISBN 1-85604-269-3

Typeset in 12/15pt Goudy Old Style and Humanist by Library Association Publishing.
Printed and made in Great Britain by Bookcraft (Bath) Ltd, Midsomer Norton, Somerset.

CONTENTS

PREFACE TO THE SECOND EDITION

The first edition of this book was written and published in 1994, just over three years ago as I write. Although *The information society* was not, in the conventional sense, a textbook, I know that it has been widely used by students, especially those on courses in information studies, librarianship and communications studies in which a broad understanding of the nature of the information society is an essential underpinning of more advanced work. That was its intended audience, although I always hoped that it would be of wider interest as well. When the time came for its second reprinting in the spring of 1997 parts of it were already out of date. Hence we decided on a second edition.

The revisions for this edition reflect the original aim of the book. The fundamental argument and structure remain intact. They grew out of the belief that we cannot understand the so-called 'information society', which will take us into the twenty-first century, unless we have some understanding of how information has been accumulated, analysed and disseminated in the past. We have to distinguish between comparatively superficial changes, which are merely technical, and the great shifts in the paradigm of human communications that have taken place three times in the history of mankind. The third of those shifts has created – and is still creating – the information society. The pace of change is unprecedented; one new feature of this edition, for example, is a discussion of the World Wide Web, now the dominant format of the Internet but still in its infancy in the early 1990s. The Internet itself is one of the key *loci* of the paradigm shift, although its growth will soon peak: if the present rate of increase in users were sustained, the number of users would exceed the total population of the world in less than a decade!

This is, however, a study of continuity as well as change, and much of what I wrote in the preface to the first edition remains true:

This book has its distant origin in lectures that I gave for some years to first-year undergraduates in the Department of Information and Library Studies at Loughborough University. In a sense, that defines its intended audience. I hope that it will be useful to those who are beginning to study librarianship and information science by suggesting some of the historical, social, political and economic context for their subject. It is not, however, a textbook, although I have added a note on further reading, which suggests other sources which will augment the factual infrastructure upon which this book rests. What I have written is an attempt to introduce students coming fresh to the field to some aspects and implications of the information society.

The starting-point is the past, and briefly the very remote past, for which I make no apology. Although much of this book is concerned with the implications of technologies that are still in a dynamic, and perhaps early, stage of development, the society on which they are impacting is very old. Computers and computer networks, for example, are merely the latest expression of the fundamental human desire to record and to communicate information. It is only in the longer historical perspective that we can begin to understand both the enormity and the limitations of what is happening now and what we are trying to do. In this context, I have attempted to examine some of the traditional systems of information provision – by publishers and by authors – as well as by librarians, and to suggest ways in which they are being challenged and modified by the use of information technology.

At the same time, I have, I hope, not made the mistake of assuming that all the changes that we are now experiencing can be characterized simply as developments in computing. They cannot, even though computing is indeed the principal driver of change.

The flow of information in society runs through many channels, of which the most common, and in some ways the most significant, are the mass media. Broadcasting, in particular, appears regularly in this book as an integral part of society's information infrastructure. The underlying argument, which runs throughout this book, is that new systems of information storage and communication have supplemented rather than supplanted what existed before. Just as we still use handwriting, despite the existence of so many mechanical substitutes for it (printing, typewriting, word-processing, and so on), so we shall continue to use the printed word even though many other media are available to us. We read newspapers despite the ubiquity of television. The diversity of media gives us greater power to communicate in the most effective way once we learn how to exploit it.

It is in this context that I have tried to suggest some of the issues that arise out of the problem of gaining access to the information which we can so ingeniously and efficiently store and disseminate. I have explored the benefits of the information revolution, as well as some of its consequences for those who are disadvantaged and disempowered by technological change. I have also suggested some of the political consequences of how we store and process information: how information systems can be abused as easily as they can be used. Finally, I have brought this back to the context of the provision of information through institutions and by those with professional skills in the management of both.

I hope that I have raised as many questions as I have answered; indeed, some of the questions admit of no answer. At a time of such rapid technological development, social evolution and political change, it is difficult to be certain of the present and impossible to make confident predictions about the future.

I hope, however, that at least some of what I have written here addresses issues that are of longer-term significance than today's management theory or tomorrow's technological miracle which will be forgotten next year. In essence, this book, like the lectures of which it is a remote derivative, is intended to provoke thought rather than merely to convey fact.

INTRODUCTION
The information society: myth and reality

As we approach the end of the twentieth century, people in the industrialized countries are increasingly conscious of living in a world that is profoundly and fundamentally different from that into which many of them were born. In little more than a decade, we have seen technological, economic, political and cultural change on a scale which, as a retrospective view becomes possible, is beginning to justify the use of the word 'revolution' to describe it. But revolution is a word that we associate with violence, with the storming of the Bastille or the bombardment of the Winter Palace. It has indeed been a violent decade in some places, but our revolution has only indirectly been a part of that. The revolution that began in the 1970s and is not yet complete has been at once less obvious and more far-reaching than a mere change in a regime or even in a whole political system. It has been a revolution in our way of living, which, in one way or another, has affected every human being on the planet.

The symbol of the revolution is the computer, the 'electronic brain' of the 'boffins' in science fiction films of a generation ago, which now seem far older than their 30 or 40 years. The computer is in almost every office, on most desks and in many homes. Behind the scenes, it is involved in almost everything we do, from buying our groceries to making a telephone call. Even after a century of almost continuous innovation in the technology of communication, and the invention of devices from the telephone to the television, the computer is perceived, however vaguely, as being in some way *different*. By understanding that difference, we can begin to understand the new society which the computer is creating, the revolution which it has both inspired and driven.

It is now two centuries since the last comparable revolution was at its height in Britain. The exploitation of the power of steam was creating a new economy, and in so doing reordering patterns of work, social relationships and the structure and political organization of society. The new arrangements which stabilized in the first half of the nineteenth century were recognizably the successor of what had gone before, but unmistakably different from it. Institutions that survived were changed; many vanished, and many new ones were created. The revolution through which we are now living is at least as great in its significance.

The steam engine was the motive power, both literal and metaphorical, of the industrial revolution; the computer is driving the revolution of the late twentieth century. Why has this machine become so important? What is so special about these devices that has made them the force behind changes far greater than those wrought by any other invention of our inventive century? The answer lies in their ability to simulate skills and attributes that we once thought were unique to ourselves: memory, logic, communication. Machines that are able to emulate, and in some ways to surpass, the intellectual and social capacities of those who make them are both fascinating and frightening. The virtually unlimited production and availability of such devices cannot leave any aspect of human thought and activity wholly untouched.

Communication and memory are central to the human experience. So far as we know, we are the only creatures on earth with a true sense of history, a desire and an ability to remember and analyse events in the past, and to make arrangements that allow us to record our knowledge and ideas in perpetuity, so that they can be recovered and understood by generations not yet born in societies which do not yet exist. Uniquely, we can communicate across time and space and have developed systems and devices that enable us to do so. These developments began in the dawn of human history, with the evolution of language itself (which some anthropologists would argue is the dawn of human history in any meaningful sense) and the later invention of the first systems for recording and preserving language in a material form.

The information-dependent society that is emerging from our revolution – the post-industrial revolution as some analysts call it – combines both profound change and fundamental continuity. It can only be understood in context. Part of this context is historical: the development of writing, printing and systems of communication. Part of it is economic: the means by which systems for the communication of information have become enmeshed in general systems of social and economic organization, so that information and the means of its storage and transmission have been commodified. A third part is political: commodified information is valorized by more than merely the cost of its production and distribution, for there is a real power to be derived from its possession and a loss of empowerment caused by its absence. These hypotheses about the origins, development and implications of the information society are at the heart of this book.

We begin with a historical survey, which sweeps without apology across much of the history of mankind. In that history, we observe first the development of writing, as people seek to preserve more information than their memories can hold and communicate it to those to whom they cannot speak. We trace the development of different systems of writing until one – the alphabet – emerges and supersedes almost all of the others because it is an adaptable and flexible means of preserving the languages in which we think and speak. Even the alphabet, however, cannot cope with all the concepts that the human mind can invent. Systems were developed which enabled our ancestors to record sound (as musical notation), numeric data and the relationship between them (as numbers and symbols for mathematical functions) and visual representation of size, shape and colour.

In the second phase of our history, a mechanical device – printing – was applied to the chronicling and dissemination of the information which was thus recorded. The invention of printing has been seen as a defining moment in the history of mankind. Certainly, it facilitated important changes in the organization and structure of western European culture, religion and politics, and was to be one of the instruments of European domination of almost all of the rest of the world. In the smaller world of communications, printing has another effect which we consider at length: it was the fundamental reason for the commodification of communications. A printer, we shall argue, needed more than merely skills in order successfully to practise his craft; a printer also needed both capital for the equipment with which the product was made, and distribution systems through which the product could be sold. The printed book was the first mass medium, because it was economically impossible for it to be anything else.

Out of printing, there developed the vast edifice of the publishing industry, the first significant manifestation of communications entering the world of commerce. The process of writing, producing and selling printed books was, for 400 years, the unchallenged system of communication between literate people. It became so familiar as to become a paradigm; its vocabulary and some of its customs have been imitated by the producers and consumers of very different media. In this book, the paradigm has been exploited to the full. There is a substantial analysis of the process of book publishing, and of the industry that has developed around it. This is developed as a model of commercial systems for the communication of knowledge and information, which can be applied in turn to the other media that have proliferated in the last hundred years.

The development of those other media – sound, vision, computing, and various combinations of them – is the final historical strand in this study. The history of information and communication in the last century is, in part, the history of the development of new devices and systems which have extended our power to communicate in two ways. First, they have made it faster and more efficient. Secondly, and more importantly, they have extended the scope of what can be communicated. Above all, accurate representations of visual phenomena – photography, film, video – have become a part of our daily lives. We have moved beyond text and language into the storage and communication of images of the visual world in which we actually live. Other inventions have speeded the transmission of information: the telegraph, the telephone, radio, television. These tools of communication are the building blocks of the information society.

Only at the very end of our historical story do we reach the computer, and yet as soon as we do so we can begin to see its all-pervasive effects. The computer has brought together so many of the developments of the past. It has both demanded and facil-itated the convergence of technologies, which allows us to combine computing with telecommunications and the digitization of text and image to permit almost instantaneous worldwide (and indeed extraterrestrial) transmission of data.

The historical approach in Chapters 1 and 2 is essentially an attempt to sketch the history of the storage, communication and retrieval of information, in terms of media and technology. We turn next to the economic issues that have arisen, which are becoming more acute and being more urgently addressed because of the increasing predominance of technology in the process of information provision and the delivery of information services. Information, as has already been suggested, was commodified and valorized by the invention of printing and the consequent development of an industry which used printing as its key tech-nology. Publishing – the paradigm – is in the front line of exposure to change under the impact of the information revolution. The market-place itself is being redefined and extended. Some activities traditionally associated with publishing and others traditionally associated with libraries are being disentangled and recombined. The new configurations have wide implications far beyond the boundaries of the academic world in which many of them originate. Electronic mail and electronic publishing are only two of the more obvious applications of the combination of computing and telecommunications which we broadly describe as 'information technology'.

The printed word, which has been the traditional commodity in the information market-place, has been supplemented and to a limited extent displaced throughout the present century. The information revolution encompasses all those media that communicate information to recipients. In the developed world, and indeed far beyond it, the most potent medium of all is television, the near-universal domestic source of information, entertainment and social interaction. Broadcasting, first in sound only and then in both sound and vision, has been with us for nearly 80 years. Its ability to transmit information and opinion instantaneously, with great apparent authority and directly to the home, was a force whose power was recognized before World War II and has been consistently exploited by governments, pressure groups and commercial interests ever since it was identified. Radio and television are integral to the information revolution, and yet they are also subject to it. Satellite broadcasting, which is computer-dependent, has brought a new sense of freedom to the television industry, but, like so many other developments, has also reiterated, if reiteration were needed, the need for huge capital investments to gain access to this key medium of information and influence.

It is not only the mass media that have changed the information market-place. Broadcasting is, by definition, a public activity. Information, however, is increasingly seen, in some respects, as being too valuable to be public. Stored in databases throughout the world is information with commercial potential to which access is restricted by the ability of the information-seeker to pay for it. Again a revolution is being wrought. The library is the historic paradigm of information storage and retrieval as publishing is of information marketing. Libraries, like publishers, have been in the front line of change. These changes are far from superficial; it is not just that libraries now contain a wide range of media, and are increasingly dependent upon technology both for their management and for the provision of services to users. There are far more profound economic changes, for libraries are part of the increasingly commercialized chain of information supply. Traditionally, the library was merely the customer of the publisher. Now it has the potential to be the publisher's partner in many enterprises, and librarians are reassessing their attitudes to the cost of information supply. Outside the institution of the library, information providers have few of the inhibitions that have traditionally made librarians look askance at such matters. Information has values assigned to it, and it is provided at a profit to the provider; prices are determined by the forces of the market.

It is out of these economic themes that the political themes that predominate in Chapters 5 and 6 emerge. On a global scale, there is a growing gap between the rich and the poor in access to information as in so much else. The technological developments of the last 50 years have made more information more available to more people than at any other time in human history. At the same time, however, the cost of those technologies, and the cost of gaining access to information through them, has made it often difficult and sometimes impossible for information to be obtained by its potential beneficiaries. This is the central paradox and the central political dilemma of the information revolution. As in the industrial revolution, in different ways, the benefits to the majority, encompassed in the abstraction of 'society', are being achieved partly at the expense of weaker and poorer individuals whose skills are becoming outmoded and whose earning power is consequently declining.

The revolution in the communication of information has created what is sometimes called a 'global village'. Yet instant access and instantaneous transmission depend upon a vastly expensive infrastructure of telecommunications and broadcasting systems on the part of the providers, and the acquisition of appropriate equipment (and sometimes skills) on the side of the consumers. Those who are excluded are the majority of the populations of most of the Third World and significant minorities even in richer countries. Even in the USA, the cabling of the 'information superhighway', the optic fibre network which will bring digital communications to the home, is already being politicized as the provider companies avoid poorer areas of cities to concentrate on the richer areas where demand and profits will be higher. The gap between information rich and information poor is increasingly overt.

If that gap is the wider political dimension of the information revolution, its most obvious immediate political consequence has been to change, or to threaten to change, the relationship between the state and its own citizens. Governments, like businesses, cannot function without information, and as they become more complex so do their information needs. Much of this is not only legitimate, it is both essential and benevolent. A modern state cannot function without such basic data as that provided by censuses, tax returns and electoral registers. There is, however, a debate, perhaps not yet sufficiently well articulated, about the boundaries of the legitimate information needs of a democratic state. Information about identifiable individuals is sensitive, and yet there are cases in which its dissemination, perhaps to a tightly defined group of recipients, is clearly in the public interest. In other cases, there can be no such interest, and dissemination is clearly an invasion of legitimate privacy. But there is an increasing number of less clear-cut areas, where the organs and agencies of the state are collecting information of potential great value or harm. The process of regulation – of balancing the general good against individual rights – has begun, but is still embryonic.

Historically, the state has always been a participant in the process of information transfer. It regulates the operation of the market-place through laws that control the dissemination of intellectual property, such as copyrights and patents, and also, in most cases, by exercising a certain level of moral jurisdiction through censorship. The state's role, however, like so much else, is being transformed by the information revolution. The very concept of copyright, which for 300 years has been the legal foundation-stone of the publishing industry, becomes blurred when the technology of copying is uncontrollably widely available. As the historic functions of publishers and libraries begin to converge in electronic publishing and electronic document supply services, the very nature of copyright will need to be redefined.

These three aspects of the evolution of the information society – the historical, the economic, the political – are considered in turn. Each raises its own questions, yet all are interrelated. The questions are not new, but they have all been made more urgent by the power of the computer to store, process and transmit information. In the industrialized countries it is no longer possible to conduct many of the most basic transactions of daily life without using the power of computers. Our greatest tool of information and communication is in danger of becoming our master. Much of this book is concerned with trying to define the issues thar are raised by this prospect.

Finally, there is one group of people in society who have a special role to play in the information revolution. Computer scientists and information workers are the engineers of the post-industrial revolution. More than any other group, publishers, librarians and archivists have seen their professions transformed; whole new professions have come into existence as governments, businesses, industries and institutions have struggled to reposition themselves to deal with the new technologies of information and communication. In those parts of the world where the information revolution has made its greatest impact, the information professionals are becoming a larger and larger part of the workforce as a whole. But it is not only those professionals whose lives are being profoundly changed. Patterns of work and patterns of employment are being transformed as radically now as they were in the move from an agricultural to an industrial economy 200 years ago. Manufacturing, itself, is no longer dependent upon the mass employment of labour as computer-based devices are made which can undertake the routine work of making and assembling of parts. We are living in the midst of this revolution. Those who are seeking to enter the information professions – for whom this book is principally intended – need to be able to formulate the questions to which the answers will prescribe the limits of their professional lives. Some of those questions are posed, and a few of the answers are suggested, in the rest of this book.

I

THE HISTORICAL DIMENSION
I From script to print

THE ORIGINS OF WRITING

The earliest evidence for the existence of *Homo sapiens* derives from the interpretation of archaeological and palaeontological evidence rather than from records consciously made by people themselves. Our species was already in an advanced stage of physiological and intellectual development before we began to leave a deliberate mark on the world around us. The first such marks, perhaps the first consciously created records, are the graphic representations of daily life which have been found in caves in France and elsewhere. Scholars debate the significance of these, whether they are religious, social, or merely artistic; for our purposes, their importance is that we have here the first evidence of a species which sought some means to represent the world in which it lived. It found a material on which the the representation could be recorded – the rock walls of a cave – and a medium – natural dyes – in which it could be made.

Between palaeolithic cave paintings and the first real records of human activities there are many centuries. The earliest cave paintings are generally considered to date from 40,000 years ago; even so, they embody the basic principle of meeting a perceived need by developing, or making use of, a combination of medium and material. All subsequent systems have developed from that same perception.

When complex societies began to evolve in various parts of

Asia, their very complexity forced them to consider, possibly even consciously, how that complexity could be managed. Pictorial representation, forceful as it is and important as it continues to be, is limited. While pictures can convey shapes and colours far more effectively than words, and can often give greater clarity than a verbal description of an action or a scene, they are less effective in embodying abstractions or ideas. A picture can show the shape and colour of a house but cannot state its financial value. A picture can represent the appearance of a person, but cannot show what that person is thinking. A picture can reproduce, with great accuracy, the appearance of a car, but it can neither explain how it works nor show it in motion. To preserve an image of anything other than a purely visual and static world, we need a system which allows us to express language in some representational form.

The essence of all writing systems, the oldest and still the most important means of achieving this, is that they allow language which describes the abstract to take on a concrete form, and in some cases can simulate the language even more accurately by representing its sound as well as the ideas which the sounds convey. The earliest writing systems, however, were non-alphabetic, and clearly derived from the practice of drawing pictures. The earliest history of writing is necessarily obscure, but it seems likely that it evolved in the Middle East about 5,000 years ago.

Its purpose was utilitarian. A stage of societal development had been reached in which something like a state was evolving. There were rulers and ruled. There was a social and economic order in which some were richer and more powerful than others. Wealth and power depended upon many factors, of which the most important was perhaps access to the raw materials of human survival: food and water. Those who were powerful enough to control natural resources were able to exercise control over others, whether on a small or a large scale. Men fought for the control of such resources. There were organized groups, in

which submitting to the leadership of the strongest or the clever-
est was clearly advantageous to the less strong or the less clever
if, in return, they were able to share in the resources. The gradual emergence of the concept of the state with a common ruler
and common interests led to the need for common resources. It
was this that seems to have forced the development of writing
systems.

The monarchies of the Tigris–Euphrates basin – on the bor-
ders of modern Iran and Iraq – raised taxes from their subjects in
order to sustain themselves and their actions for the common
good. As this process was regularized, it became necessary to
record what had been paid, for what purpose, and by and to
whom payment had been made. This necessitated a system
which could record quantity as well as indicate the medium in
which payment had been made. Thus if the ruler demanded a
proportion of the crop as a form of taxation (in return for the
defence of the farmer's land), the writing system had to be able
to represent the crop itself, its total size, the relationship between
that total and the farmer's liability, and the fact of payment having been made. No purely graphic system could achieve this, and
what evolved was a means of using modified pictorial images.

Corn, the most basic commodity of such a society, was represented by a symbol clearly derived in part from its appearance.
Numbers are more complicated, but even for them a form of
visual representation was possible. It was based on the fingers of
the human hand, so that a single stroke represented 'one', two
strokes 'two', and so on. Symbols could be used which described
people by their attributes, a ceremonial headdress or crown for
the king, a hoe for the peasant, and so on. A representational
writing system of this kind was limited but practical.

A writing system, however, can never be independent of the
medium in which it can be used. Such a medium, like the writing
system itself, emerges out of social necessity and environmental
circumstances. In the Tigris–Euphrates basin there is water, sand

and intense heat. Taken together, they allowed the peoples of the region to develop simple but effective mechanisms for turning mud into bricks by combining the sand and the water, and drying it in the sun. As it dried, inscriptions could easily be made in the surface of the brick, which, when it was baked, would be permanent. It is on such clay tablets that the earliest written records of mankind are to be found.

The system of writing used in the ancient Middle East is known to scholars as *cuneiform* (literally 'wedge-shaped', derived from the shape of the instrument presumably used for inscribing the symbols in the clay). Significant numbers of clay tablets containing such inscriptions have been found by archaeologists, and can be seen in museums around the world. Cuneiform, however, was not unique. Other systems evolved along similar lines elsewhere, many of them, like cuneiform, essentially derived from an attempt to use a modified form of pictorial representation of objects. Such modifications, however, still carried with them the essential disadvantages of representational systems based, however distantly, on pictorial images: an inability to convey abstractions and actions. It was possible to represent a king, but less easy to illustrate 'monarchy' or 'state'. Some writing systems achieved this by using the image of an object (a crown to represent 'king') to mean the abstraction which the object itself symbolized or embodied (a crown to represent 'sovereignty'). The script which began to be developed in China in about 1500 BC became particularly adept at this. Characters for objects could even be combined to represent a concept associated with the combination.

The transition from purely pictorial systems (*pictographs*) to systems which combined pictographs and characters for more abstract concepts (*hieroglyphs*) took place independently in China and in Egypt. Neither pictographs nor hieroglyphs, however, really address the central problem of the representation of language. Language evolved as sounds, and different languages use sounds in different ways. Some sounds, or phonemes, which are common in some languages are unknown in others; the 'th' sound in words like 'the' in English does not exist in French, and is as notoriously difficult to a native speaker of French as the French 'r' and 'u' sounds (as in '*rue*') are to native English speakers. Words used to describe objects, actions or attributes are merely commonly understood combinations of sounds. The word 'house' has no absolute meaning any more than '*maison*' has; it merely happens, through a process of development over many centuries, that these two random combinations of sound have come to signify the same object to speakers of different languages. By going behind what is signified by words to the sounds of which the words are constituted, we reach the raw material of language itself.

The realization of this, whether consciously or unconsciously, led to the next stage in the development of writing systems: the use of symbols to represent sounds. The earliest systems, known as *syllabaries*, took the phoneme, or unit of pronunciation, as their building blocks. The 'th' combination is a phoneme in English, but not in French, where the juxtaposition of the two letters is pronounced quite differently. Phonemes could only be represented symbolically, since they were derived from sounds, not objects. Syllabaries broke the link between visual representation and the representation of human speech. The Chinese pictographs, for example, having been adopted by the Japanese, were modified by them and eventually replaced by a syllabary in which each symbol represents a phoneme. Thus symbols can be combined and recombined to form the visual representation of words, regardless of the meaning of the words themselves.

THE ALPHABET

Although the syllabary could be argued to be a more advanced writing system than hieroglyphs or pictographs, it was still limited in its applications. Where phonemes vary between languages, each language needs its own character set to represent them. Only by breaking the phonemes into even more basic units can the final flexibility be achieved. It was in the Middle East, yet again, that this final stage of development took place, about 3,000 years ago. The Phoenicians, a trading people living on the eastern shores of the Mediterranean, developed a form of representing speech which eliminated all pictorial images and almost all representations of phonemes. The Greek alphabet derived directly from this and in that script the phonemes all but vanished. The few survivors, such as θ (theta, the English 'th' sound as in 'the'), are conspicuous by being unusual. For all practical purposes, the ancient Greeks used an alphabet just as we do. A variation of the Greek alphabet, eliminating the remaining phonemic characters, was developed by the Romans, and survives today as our 'Roman' or 'Latin' alphabet, the alphabet in which nearly all European languages are written.

The Latin alphabet is not, however, unique. Greek still survives. Moreover, it was modified by early Christian missionaries to represent some of the Slavic languages of eastern Europe, and in this form, as Cyrillic, it is in use for Russian, Ukrainian, Bulgarian and other languages of the region. Another branch of the original Middle Eastern alphabet developed differently among the speakers of Semitic languages, and became Hebrew and Arabic. All these various developments have one essential feature in common: the adaptability to different languages which have different phonemes. Thus the Latin alphabet can be used for English, French, German, and so on, with only minor modifications (such as the use of accents). Cyrillic is also used for several languages. Arabic script is used for Urdu and for other languages in western Asia; a modified form of the Pali script of India is used for the quite different Thai language, and so on. Even more remarkably, languages can change from one script to another. Turkish used to be written in Arabic script, but since

1924 has been written in the Latin alphabet. In many Asian countries, transliteration of public notices, road signs, and the like are a common sight to aid the western visitor. Many of the languages of Africa and the islands of the Pacific, never reduced to writing by their native speakers, can be written only in the Latin characters introduced by colonial conquerors and missionaries. An alphabet is an almost infinitely flexible tool for the representation of language, and hence for its storage and transmission.

The survival of the Latin alphabet after the dissolution of the western half of the Roman Empire in the fifth century is one of the key events in the cultural history of Europe. It was the alphabet in which the sacred writings of the Christian Church were written in the West, as well as being a link with the fading memories of Rome's former glories which were still seen as a model of good government and vibrant culture. The alphabet was used when the languages of the new rulers of western Europe, the tribes of the east and the north, began to write their languages, and thus became the alphabet of the emerging western vernaculars. Those northern languages which had evolved their own syllabaric systems, such as the runes used for Norse, rapidly succumbed. The common alphabet has preserved and embodied something of the cultural unity of the west for 1,500 years, and allowed westerners to learn each other's languages with comparative ease. The absence of a common language has been less problematic than it might have been because of the existence of a common alphabet.

The central role of an alphabet in the storage and communication of information cannot be overstated. In essence, it permits the representation in permanent and commonly understood form of a multiplicity of languages, and hence of any concept which can be expressed in the languages which it represents. It minimizes the obstacles to understanding, is easy to learn, easy to use and readily adaptable. It is not, however, perfect.

In moving to the greater flexibility of alphabetic systems, there were losses as well as gains. The hunting scenes so vividly portrayed by the cave artists can be described in words only with great difficulty and inevitable loss of impact. Colour, sound and some actions are notoriously difficult to describe. No words can express the concept of 'red' to a sightless or colour-blind person, or the concept of 'loud' to a person with no hearing, any more than we can see 'good' or hear 'light'. Moreover, human sensory abilities vary from person to person. To those with perfect pitch, the mere words 'middle C' convey a precise sound which they can 'hear' and perhaps reproduce vocally; to others it may conjure up a visual image of a particular note on the keyboard of a piano, or of a piece of musical notation; to some, it will mean nothing at all. Both knowledge and ability limit our capacity to understand the concepts represented by alphabetic symbols made into words; there are, therefore, limits to the usefulness of the alphabetic symbols themselves.

IMAGES, SOUNDS AND NUMBERS

The visual representation of objects, colours and shapes has always been an integral part of human culture. As we have seen, it was the first aspect of human experience to be recorded in a permanent form, and except when representational art has been banned for cultural reasons (as in some Islamic traditions, for example) it has never ceased to exist. Visual imagery has, however, gradually extended beyond simply representing what can be seen. Map-making was perhaps the first example of this. The ancient geographers drew patterns which illustrated their understanding of the shape of geographical features, but they did so in a way which they could not possibly have seen. Until well into the twentieth century, almost no human being had ever risen far enough above the surface of the earth to be able to see the shapes of coastlines, for example, or the courses of rivers. Maps have always been made by using conventions of signs and symbolism to represent what is believed to exist but cannot be seen as a whole. The conventions, and the techniques behind them, have changed, but the essential principle has remained the same.

The alphabet embodies a key principle of the communication of information: the need for a means to represent language in a permanent and generally understood form. A map takes this one stage further: the communication of information by the visual representation of that which has to be deduced because it can be neither described in language, nor verified by visual observation. Alphabetic and visual information recording systems cannot, however, embody the whole range of human communications. Language embodies thought and speech; pictorial images, whether realistically or symbolically representational embody what we can see; but we also hear things other than speech. Some non-speech sounds can indeed be alphabetically represented; we can describe a dog as 'barking', a word which signifies, although it does not represent, the sound which the animal makes. We can even try to represent the sound made by the dog as 'woof' or some similar attempt at an onomatopoeic word. No words, however, can convey the sounds of the wind, birdsong or music, and for the latter in particular, a whole series of systems of notation have been developed to allow composers to represent their wishes in a way that is comprehensible to performers. Musical notation, like the symbols on a map, is a recording system which acts as a surrogate for, and works similarly to, an alphabet, in a situation in which the alphabet is inadequate because language itself is inadequate.

Most difficult of all is the representation of quantitative data. Measurement was a concept which was highly developed in the very societies in which the earliest writing systems were developed, but none entirely solved the problem of the representation of numbers and of calculations in which numbers were used. The Greeks developed a vastly complicated system using alphabetic characters, as did the Romans, but even the latter's was almost impossibly clumsy for all but the most elementary mathematical applications. It was the Arabs who finally solved the problem, developing ten symbols to represent the numerals from one to nine and (crucially) zero, and the now universal symbols to represent the basic functions of addition, subtraction, multiplication and division. Mathematical symbols, like musical notation, are a substitute for the alphabet used to convey concepts for which language is inadequate or inappropriate.

THE FIRST MEDIA

All these various systems of representing information, whether linguistic, numeric, visual or aural, depend on the existence not only of a means of representation – a system of recording – but also of a means of preserving the representation, that is a form of recording medium. The earliest media were natural substances, such as rock, bone or wood. The rock of the cave was unmodified from its natural form unless the surface was washed or prepared in some other way before the painter set to work. Other 'natural' media were, however, changed, sometimes quite significantly. Bone, for example, which is the medium on which the oldest Chinese characters are preserved, had to be cleaned and perhaps polished or planed before it could be used. Similarly, wood had to be prepared by cutting, planing and perhaps sizing. Even the 'natural' media, therefore, were actually the products of human ingenuity and skill, just like the recording systems which they were designed to carry.

The baked clay tablets of the Assyrians were to prove to be more typical than wood or bone for the future development of media. Different societies evolved different media according to their needs, their technological capacity and the availability of materials. Indeed, in many cultures different media were used for different purposes. The ancient Romans, for example, continued to use stone for monumental inscriptions (as we do ourselves) long after papyrus, vellum and parchment had become common; the choice between the latter three was determined partly by purpose and partly by economic considerations. Similarly, the Egyptians painted and inscribed hieroglyphs even after they developed a syllabary that could more conveniently be written on papyrus or parchment.

The important thing about recording media is that they should be appropriate. Appropriateness is not an absolute concept, but it can be broadly defined in terms of suitability for purpose. An inscription on stone, which can be made only by a highly skilled person over a comparatively long period of time and which can be neither modified nor easily transported, is clearly quite unsuitable for some casual purpose such as making a note of domestic accounts or an *aide-mémoire* of a course of action which has been agreed. Cultures therefore evolve different media for different purposes. For most of the recording systems which we have already discussed, what was needed is a smooth surface on which symbols can be inscribed, written or painted. In turn this requires some kind of implement, and (for writing and painting), a substance which can be applied to the surface. The familiar version of this is of pen, ink and paper, all of which have existed, in some form or other, for many centuries.

The most useful media for writing are, literally, the most flexible. Clay tablets, polished stone, bones, wood bark and similar surfaces are solid, but clumsy. They take up a great deal of storage space, and some of them (clay and wood, for example) deteriorate rapidly or (like bone or baked clay) are easily damaged. A strong flexible surface, on the other hand, can be easily stored (by rolling or folding) and is less susceptible to damage, although far from permanent in some cases. In western Asia, in the first millennium BC, various kinds of vegetable matter and animal derivatives were used to make such materials. The papyrus reed, which grows in the shallows along the banks of the Nile in Egypt and Sudan, could easily be processed into a reasonably good writing material, which, although a little fragile if it was bent, could be sewn into large sheets, and could be rolled for storage if it were treated carefully. The surface, when sized, would hold ink without blotting, and the raw material itself was readily available. Papyrus became one of the most common writing materials in the eastern Mediterranean towards the end of the first millennium BC.

The alternative to vegetable matter was to use suitably processed animals skins. When stripped from the flesh of a dead beast, cleaned of its hair, and partially tanned, the hide of the cow, goat or camel could be turned into a very effective writing surface. Like papyrus, it could hold the ink, and was stronger in several senses. Vellum and parchment are less susceptible to damp than is papyrus, and can also be folded as well as rolled. This was to be of particular importance as the modern form of the book began to evolve in the first and second centuries AD.

THE DEVELOPMENT OF THE BOOK

The development of the familiar form of the book is a defining moment in the history of information storage and retrieval in the West, as important in its way as the invention of the alphabet. Until about the beginning of the Christian Era, written documents were either single sheets, stored (if at all) flat, or long scrolls of sheets of papyrus, vellum or parchment, sewn or glued together end to end. These were stored in cylindrical cases, made of wood or metal, of which examples have been found among the petrified ruins of Pompeii, and which are still used for ceremonial purposes in storing the scriptures in Jewish liturgical rites.

Towards the end of the first century BC, small sheets of parchment held together with a single thread at the corner began to be used as informal notebooks, and it was from these that the modern form of the book (the *codex*) was gradually developed over a period of about a century. A key stage in this development was when the sewing together of single sheets was replaced by the folding of the sheets before sewing, creating a codex which was at once simpler and stronger. It seems that the development of the codex was particularly associated with the Christians, perhaps because they needed portable books which could easily be concealed for their missionary activities in the Roman Empire. When Christianity became the established religion of the Empire in the early fourth century AD, the scroll came to be associated with the pagan past. The codex proved so convenient that it even triumphed as a medium for the pagan classics.

The general adoption of the codex is a perfect example of the acceptance of an information storage medium which is both effective and appropriate. Easy to make, easy to store and easy to use, the codex had every possible advantage over the scroll. Its cultural, religious and ultimately political overtones simply served to make it even more acceptable. Like the alphabet, once Europe had adopted the codex it never abandoned it, and it was to become one of the symbols of European influence in the non-European world from the fifteenth century onwards.

The codex proved to have a longer active life than the materials from which the first codices were made. Vellum and parchment were both ultimately replaced by paper, while papyrus could never be used for codices at all because of its fragility when folded. Paper, unlike papyrus, is a product which undergoes a long and complicated manufacturing process during which the vegetable fibres from which it is made are physically and chemically modified. They are reduced to a pulp with water, and then reconstituted by drying in flat sheets. When the surface is sized, the material can take ink, and the sheet be unfolded or rolled, and, provided that the materials are reasonably free of chemical impurities and the conditions of storage are reasonably good, it can be stored for long periods of time.

Paper was invented in China at the beginning of the fifth century AD, and the use of it, and the knowledge of the craft of paper-making, spread gradually westwards during the next thousand years. At first it came along the ancient trade routes that linked east and west across the steppes and mountains of what are now the states of central Asia. It reached western Asia at the time of the great Arab cultural expansion in the first century of Islam, and was taken by the Arabs throughout their burgeoning Empire in North Africa and southern Europe. From Spain and Italy it made its way northwards, until, by the fifteenth century, paper-making and the use of paper was well established throughout southern and western Europe. On the whole, however, it was used for less formal purposes; for formal or important documents, vellum or parchment were still common.

The alphabet, the codex and paper proved to be a formidable combination as an information storage and retrieval system. This was even more true when they were combined with a new system of 'writing' the alphabet on the paper. Writing was a manual process, whether the implement was a stylus, a chisel, a brush or a pen. In China, in the eleventh century AD, a form of printing had been invented which involved making reproductions from engraved wooden blocks, a format particularly suited to the vast number of pictographs and syllabaries which, by that time, formed the Chinese character set. The process was adopted in Korea (which used a similar character set), but spread no further, and seems to have remained unknown in the West.

PRINTING: THE FIRST COMMUNICATIONS REVOLUTION

Printing in Europe was invented separately, in the fifteenth century. The earliest experiments may have been with wooden blocks, but the breakthrough was the realization that the languages written in the Latin alphabet could be printed using only a very small number of characters. The inventor of typographic printing was Johann Gutenberg, a German goldsmith who, with various financial backers, printed the first European book, an edition of the Bible in Latin (1454–5). Gutenberg invented devices for making type as multiple copies of individual raised letters on the upper surface of small pieces of lead, and also various techniques for combining these, applying ink to them and imprinting their image on a suitable surface. The most suitable surface soon proved to be paper. The invention of printing sounded the death knell of parchment and vellum as the normal material for books and documents in Europe.

The rapid spread of the art of printing marked the beginning of a period of profound, even revolutionary, cultural change in the West. Printed books could be produced in great quantities, and were therefore both more widely available and cheaper than their hand-made predecessors. Moreover, every copy of the same edition was identical with every other copy, which allowed a whole series of aids to the use of books to be developed: the index, the citation, the bibliographical record. Because paper was so easy to use for books, and so comparatively strong and adaptable, formats became smaller, books became lighter and more portable and hence even cheaper and even more convenient. The codex itself survived as the normal form of the western book.

The written word, in printed form, became an integral part of life for the first time, a fact whose importance cannot be overemphasized. Print was an apparently far more stable medium than manuscript, and certainly more uniform. It was used by rulers and rebels alike in every sphere of life. No subject of the king could claim to be ignorant of the law when laws were accurately and identically disseminated in printed form. A religious or political rebel could reach a far larger audience when ideas could be circulated in print than had ever been possible when the range was limited either by personal contact and speech or by the limited production of handwritten copies. Scholars could read the work of other scholars whom they would never meet, and could study the very sources which had been used when an identical printed version lay upon the desks in front of them. Print transformed the cultural, religious and political life of Europe.

The tradition of learning which western Europe had inherited from the ancient world was essentially repetitive rather than critical. Partly under the influence of the Church, which was paramount in all intellectual life for more than a thousand years, enquiry and experimentation was discouraged. Each generation learned what a previous generation had learned before, and little was added to the store of human knowledge and understanding. Originality was discouraged, and if it was achieved its dissemination could easily be prevented. Printing changed that forever. It became possible to compare, to contrast and to analyse on a far greater scale. Variant texts of sacred and secular works alike could be edited and reconciled into a standard, accepted, version, which anyone could read and criticize. Scholars who, before the invention of printing, might never have seen more than a few score books in their lives, could now consult libraries containing thousands of books, printed throughout Europe, and written by those who, like themselves, had ever easier access to the growing store of knowledge. Printing provoked the first information explosion.

To contain, exploit and control the potential of print, new mechanisms and new institutions had to be devised. Containment was indeed barely possible. Both secular and ecclesiastical authorities throughout Europe tried to clamp down on printing, but it spread inexorably across the continent. If it could not be suppressed, it could, however, be controlled; censorship by Church and State was an integral part of the world of the printed word almost from its very beginning. Exploitation could take many forms. Those who were censors could use the new medium to propagate their own views, and they did so shamelessly, both in Church and State. Indeed, the very idea of the centralized, bureaucratized, nation-state developed in parallel with the spread of printing. But there was another form of exploitation, perhaps more positive, which gave more people access to books and information. After the great religious divide between Protestant and Catholic in the middle of the sixteenth century, one group − the Protestants − emphasized the need for literacy. In turn, this led to the creation of new and more inclusive systems of education, and the foundation of libraries, great and small, through which a new educated elite could be created. The process proved unstoppable once it had started, and as print became more integrated into the life of the West, literacy ceased to be a luxury and became a necessity. The invention of printing started all of this and more, demonstrating perhaps for the first time, the power which accrues to those who control and have access to information and the concomitant disadvantage of those who do not. Knowledge became cumulative, as each generation added to the store, and recorded its findings and its opinions in a permanent and easily retrievable form, which at last began to realize the full potential of the alphabet as a means of storing linguistic information.

Printing technology was designed for reproducing alphabetic systems, and is less suitable for other forms of representation. The pictographic and syllabaric scripts of Asia have always presented a problem to printers, a fact which had important consequences as Europe began to impose its cultural domination on much of the rest of the world. Musical notation and even mathematical symbols similarly presented difficulties (although by no means insuperable ones) to printers, and the reproduction of graphic matter remained a problem for 300 years after the death of Gutenberg. In other words, despite its obvious advantages, printing was a limited medium, but because of its ubiquity, it turned western Europe into a culture dominated by what it could do so easily: reproduce written language. Oral culture, although never entirely lost, was submerged, and both the visual and the aural became parallel and separate experiences from the linguistic. Hence literacy, which had to be acquired by learning, became the basic skill of the western elite, while the more natural skills of seeing and hearing were, to some extent, devalued as mechanisms for information transfer.

For 400 years, printing was the dominant information transfer medium, and for much of that time was unchallenged. Perhaps for that very reason, further development of the technology was slow. Mechanical power (first steam and then electricity) was applied to the printing press itself in the nineteenth century, and machine processes replaced handcrafts in paper-making at the same time, but it was not until the twentieth century that mechanical systems entirely displaced typesetting by hand, and there are, to this day, some hand processes in the binding of books. The intense conservatism of the book-making industry – paper-making, printing and binding – reflects the unassailable position which the industry has occupied in the storage and dissemination of information for almost the whole of its history.

THE TRADE IN BOOKS

The dominance of print also had economic consequences. The gradual evolution of both religious and secular writing in the cultures bordering on the Mediterranean, and further east in both India and China, had, over many centuries, increased the knowledge of reading and writing, and gradually brought it closer to the commercial arena. In Greece, books were undoubtedly bought and sold, and in Rome, by the first century BC, there was a flourishing trade in books. They were copied by professional scriveners, sold by booksellers, and even commissioned by 'publishers'. The book trade, such as it was, vanished with the Roman Empire in the West, but it survived in Byzantium, and independently re-emerged in Paris in the twelfth century. In due

course, in many western cities, professional scribes copied manu-
scripts for students and scholars, and soon for a few secular customers as well, so that by the middle of the fifteenth century
there was an established book trade in almost all the larger
towns of western Europe.

It may well be that it was the demand for books generated by
this trade that motivated Gutenberg and others to experiment
with a mechanical means which would replace the slow and
tedious process of writing by hand every book which was
required by a customer. Whether or not this was the case (and it
seems likely that it was), the fact remains that the printed book
was born into a world in which books were already indissolubly
linked with commerce. The process of printing itself ensured that
the link could never be broken. Even at the simplest level, a
printer needed type, ink, a press and paper, as well as the necessary skills to make use of them. From the beginning, the printing
trade needed capital investment, which could only be recouped
over the medium-term by the sale of the product. This taught
harsh lessons to some printers; Gutenberg was not only the first
typographic printer, he was also the first printer to go bankrupt.

Books produced in such unprecedentedly large numbers could
not find a large enough market where they were produced, as the
products of commercial scriptoria normally had. A bookselling
network developed throughout western and southern Europe,
based on existing trade routes and trade fairs, which, by the middle of the sixteenth century had established a system of book distribution which allowed books to travel from one end of the
continent to the other with little commercial impediment. This
served to emphasize the book as an object of commerce, and the
information that it contained, therefore, as having some monetary value. The book trade, as it spread across Europe, and vastly
increased in size, especially in the nineteenth century, became a
massive contributor to economic as well as to cultural life.

The enmeshment of the printed word in the development of

capitalist economies inevitably put another obstacle between many people and information which they wanted or needed. By the nineteenth century, and in some cases earlier, social and political reformers recognized that they could only reach the masses through the printed word if the forms of print were cheap enough for them to buy and common enough to justify the time and effort of learning to read and sustaining their literacy. Education, book provision and political change became closely associated in the minds of many radicals from the seventeenth century onwards, but never more so than during the nineteenth century when the partial mechanization of the printing industry brought the price of books and newspapers down to realistic levels for less wealthy buyers and readers. At the same time, governments used fiscal devices as a form of censorship, taxing newspapers and other reading matter in an attempt to prevent the wide circulation of radical ideas. Although this policy was gradually abandoned from the middle of the century onwards in many countries in western Europe, both taxation and formal censorship survived in many other parts of the world.

The nineteenth century saw the high point of the dominance of western culture by print. A combination of economic, technical, social and political circumstances made the printed word seem to be the unique instrument of cultural enrichment and change. No other medium could challenge its capacity to record and reproduce information, while the printed book was a uniquely efficient instrument of information retrieval. Great libraries of such books were the store houses of the world's knowledge, whether in private hands or accessible to a wider public. Yet even as print achieved these pinnacles, the process of displacement began.

Even at the height of its domination, print never displaced the spoken word as the most common means of human communication and information transfer. Orality has always been a parallel skill to literacy, and for most people, throughout most of history, far more important. Much of the knowledge that we need in our daily lives has been acquired orally and by example, from the simplest skills which we were taught as children to the immense complexity of the use of language itself. Even as a formal mechanism for the transmission of information, orality was never entirely displaced. The lecture survived (perhaps for too long) the invention of the textbook. The spoken word was integral to the development of democratic processes, looking back to the partially pre-literate societies of Greece and Rome. In a society in which illiteracy was common (as it was in much of the West until the last quarter of the nineteenth century) orality remained an essential tool of social intercourse and social control, but if language was to be preserved it had to be written down and perhaps printed.

2

THE HISTORICAL DIMENSION
2 Mass media and new technology

THE PICTORIAL IMAGE

During the second half of the nineteenth century, there began the second great revolution in the storage and communication of information. It can be seen as an attempt to overcome some of the inflexibility of print, tied as it was to the alphabetic representation of language and a few other sets of symbols such as those used by musicians or mathematicians. The earliest experiments were with processes that facilitated the reproduction of visual images in print. Such processes had existed since the fifteenth century, and indeed the simplest of them – the carved wooden block – had probably been invented in Europe before typographic printing and had certainly been in use in east Asia for centuries before the first book was printed in the West. Woodcuts were crude but could be effective; indeed the woodcuts that allegedly illustrated the martyrdom of English Protestants in the reign of Mary I became one of the most common visual images of the past for millions of people in the following 200 years.

At a more sophisticated and technically satisfying level, a printing process that made it possible to reproduce engravings made on metal (usually copper) plates, was developed in the sixteenth century. This process was in use, with some modifications and refinements, for 200 years; engravers reached a high level of technical and artistic achievement. At the very end of the eighteenth century, another new printing process, lithography, made it possible for the artist to draw an image on a prepared block of stone (or later of metal) which could then be reproduced without any further intervention from an engraver or woodcutter. However, all of these processes, even woodcut, were expensive, and, except in the very best of hands, reproductions were little more than approximations to the subjects they allegedly portrayed.

From the 1840s onwards, the invention of photography changed this forever. Although the early processes were expensive, cumbersome and unreliable, within 30 years a means had been found of reproducing photographs in print. By the end of the century they were beginning to appear in some of the more popular newspapers. Long before then, photographs of famous places and people had become a part of daily life, quite apart from the use of photography for more personal purposes as an expensive, but increasingly common, hobby. Photography created a new view of the world. A photograph was assumed to be accurate, and it allowed people to 'see' things that they would never see in reality, without any mediation or interpretation by an artist or an engraver. This directness, however, was more apparent than real. Photography, like most of the media that followed it, required operators with technical skills not only in the creation of the image itself but also in processing it to make it visible to the viewer. Photography did nevertheless open up another aspect of the world, just as printing had done 400 years earlier, for like printing, it overcame some of the barriers of time and distance in the transmission of information. It had its own inherent technical and economic obstacles to the full exploitation of its potential. Photography nevertheless began the revolution in visual information.

THE RECORDING AND TRANSMISSION OF SOUND

The invention of recording and the development of telegraphy and wireless gave a vastly greater significance to orality. At first, sound recording was little more than a rich person's toy, used almost entirely for the recording of music. The problem of transmitting sound over distance needed to be resolved in a different way. The first electro-mechanical device to achieve this was the electric telegraph invented in 1844. Its coded messages, important as they were in government, business and news gathering, could never have the same immediacy of impact as voice transmission, but telegraph cables were laid all over Europe and North America, and ultimately between continents, to provide the first system of instantaneous communication over distances beyond the limits of human vision. The telephone (invented in 1876) was a great advance on the telegraph, by allowing direct spoken communication. By the end of the nineteenth century, it was becoming common in north America, and beginning to be used in Europe.

The telephone, like photography, was for the rich, although it was always more than a social toy. The obvious use of both telegraphy and telephony in business and in government made them a matter of public concern as photography had never been. The obvious potential of both systems made them as interesting to late nineteenth-century governments as printing had been to the authorities of early sixteenth-century Europe. Just as the bishops and princes of the Renaissance had reacted to printing by censoring the printed word, the governments of the later nineteenth century reacted to the invention of the telegraph and telephone by developing state-owned or state-controlled networks of cables and exchanges and even equipment. In most countries this did not lead to censorship, although in a few it did, but everywhere it opened up the possibility of monitoring telephone telephone conversations. Only in the USA was a purely commercial telephone system permitted, but even there the companies were partially regulated under federal and state laws. Around the world, two forms of regulation were developed: the American model, which involved the state only as regulator, and the other, common in Europe, which involved state ownership of the infrastructure of telecommunications. In Britain, telephones were a virtual monopoly of the Post Office almost from their first introduction until the 1980s; this pattern was replicated in many countries.

MASS MEDIA: RADIO AND CINEMA

Wireless broadcasting was the second great contributor to the development of the oral communications culture of the twentieth century. Another invention of the late nineteenth century, it had two basic uses. It could be used for communications from one person to another, rather like a telephone but with a different technology, or it could be used for communication from one person to many people, provided that all of the would-be recipients of the signal had appropriate equipment on which to receive it. It was the latter principle – broadcasting – that was to become of paramount importance. Wireless broadcasting of both speech and music was established in western Europe and North America by the mid-1920s (and earlier in some countries) and rapidly became an integral part of daily life. Here there was indeed a formidable challenge to the primacy of print on many fronts. The broadcasters could at the same time beat the printed newspapers in the immediacy of their coverage and occupy the leisure time that might otherwise have been devoted to reading books. Broadcasting could be used for education, as well as for entertainment and information. It gave politicians and others a new means of reaching those whom they wished to influence. In some countries, broadcasting became a prime medium for advertising, and in others for political and religious propaganda. Some governments took charge of this powerful new medium, and carefully controlled access to it. Some developed regulatory regimes which tried to protect the independence of the broadcasters and a few allowed it into an almost entirely commercial sphere. Everywhere, however, the potency and influence of the new medium was recognized and acknowledged.

The commercial success of sound broadcasting meant that it was possible to manufacture receivers at a price that large numbers of people could afford. The wireless (it did not become the 'radio' in popular speech in Britain until the 1960s) took its place in almost every western home during the 1930s. It became a vital instrument of information and opinion-forming before and during World War II.

The other great popular medium of that period, although one which was perhaps used more for entertainment than for information, was the cinema. Moving pictures had first been made in the 1890s, and a small industry had begun to develop around their production and distribution before World War I. By 1920, the centre of that industry was the USA, although a number of European countries, including Britain, continued to be serious players in the market. From the mid-1920s onwards, however, American money, talent and ideas dominated the cinema throughout the world except where governments tried to prevent or limit the import or exhibition of American films. The addition of sound to the formerly silent images (which were in fact always accompanied by live music in the cinema) in 1927 completed the creation of a new and powerful information medium. Film was to be one of the most potent mechanisms for propaganda in the 1930s and World War II in both the democracies and the dictatorships.

These new media were beginning to undermine both the primacy of print itself and the cultural self-confidence of its advocates by the end of the 1930s. The pleasure to be obtained from listening to the radio or watching a film was, for many people, as great as or greater than that from reading a book, and perhaps demanded less effort and fewer skills. Information acquired through a broadcast or a film was similarly 'easy'; it soon came to be regarded as being as authoritative as the printed word. The new media, however, were monolithic in a way in which the printed word had never been, at least in comparatively open societies. Even in the democracies, the economics of both broadcasting and film-making effectively dictated the creation of monopolies or near-monopolies. The British compromise of a politically independent public sector monopoly broadcaster was a model that found no significant imitators. Even in Britain, it could not be applied to the cinema with its dependence on American suppliers of films. The infrastructure of both broadcasting and cinema was so expensive that only the very rich, or large well-capitalized companies, could truly compete in the mass market. In both production and distribution in the film industry, it was the large-scale capitalists who succeeded, and thus were born the media giants which characterize so much of the global communications and information industry at the end of the twentieth century.

TELEVISION

Influential as they were, sound broadcasting and the cinema had their limitations. The former made its impact by being instantaneous (and sometimes even spontaneous, though rarely so in Britain) and in the home; the latter did so by its use of powerful visual images, emotive music and evocation of a lifestyle far beyond the reach of the vast majority of its audience. Television, the last and greatest of the mass media, did both. It was at once domestic and universal, instantaneous and ubiquitous. From very tentative beginnings in 1936, television became, within little more than 30 years, the most universal and most powerful medium of communication and information ever invented. Like radio, it could be used and misused by governments and commercial interests alike. It could also, however, convey images of potent immediacy, whether of an assassination or a football match. It has irreversibly changed the way in which human beings live throughout the world, and how that world is perceived.

Like radio and the cinema, television broadcasting needs a complex and costly infrastructure, although in real terms, the cost began to fall in the 1980s as new miniaturized and digitized technologies became widely available. In practice, however, there has been limited opportunity for competition in the television industry. Even countries which have a fundamentally free market, such as the USA, also have a regulatory regime and some control over output. In most western countries, state broadcasters compete with the private sector, sometimes funded by advertising for which they also have to compete. Only in the late 1980s, with the global spread of satellite and cable systems, did a serious element of uncontrolled competition enter into the television industry. For most of its history so far, television has emphasized and probably hastened the development of monopolistic commercial control of the communication of information.

Taken together, the mass media of the twentieth century have enriched and enhanced the lives of hundreds of millions of people throughout the world. Despite the foreboding of moralists, the fears of governments and the complaints of a partially displaced cultural elite (all of them with some justification), cinema, radio and, above all, television, have given more access to more information to more people than at any time in history. Moreover, the traditional information industry of the printed word has survived the assault. It has changed, perhaps fundamentally (a theme that will be further explored in Chapter 3), but all the various media, including print, have a role in the global information and communication economy. As we begin to be able to develop an historical perspective, we can perhaps see that the mass media of the twentieth century have supplemented rather than displaced the printed word. They do best the things which it does badly or not at all: they have visual and aural impact, they have immediacy, they have ease of access, they have universality. Together, the mass media have revived and extended the oral and visual culture which was almost lost in the world of print. Even those who are regular readers now absorb much of their knowledge of current affairs from radio and television, and newspapers have adapted themselves accordingly. Musical performances, sporting events, even the proceedings of parliaments, which were once directly available only to the few, and could reach the majority only in a reported form, are now directly visible and audible to almost everyone. If it can be argued that print began the process of democratization in Europe, it can be as cogently suggested that the mass media have the potential to complete that process throughout the world.

COMPUTERS: THE THIRD COMMUNICATIONS REVOLUTION

The mass media supplement print, and have displaced only its less effective applications. The same may not be quite so true of the effects of the third revolution, that based on the use of computers. Attempts to make mechanical devices to assist in mathematical calculations are almost as old as mathematics itself. The abacus was widely used in China a thousand years ago, and is still in use there today. Most famously, in the middle of the nineteenth century, Charles Babbage designed, but never built, what he called a 'difference engine' in which the movements of mechanical parts were determined by logical sequences which followed from the operation of particular keys. Babbage's engine might not even have worked, but it did incorporate the essential principle of building a machine which would respond in a predetermined (or 'programmed') way to a particular set of circumstances. The means of building such a machine did not exist until the middle of the twentieth century.

The impetus for its creation came from the impact of war in the 1940s. The need to break the codes used by the Germans for their military wireless traffic forced British scientists to develop machines that could take strings of apparently meaningless letters and find the logical sequences which had to exist if the signal had any meaning The machines that were ultimately developed to do this were also capable of being programmed to undertake mathematical calculations and other logical operations. The writing and application of logical programs was, and remains, the basis of computing. There have, however, been two great changes. The first is the storage capacity of the computers themselves – their ability to 'remember' information – and their capacity to process the information which is held in the memory. The second is the development of a linkage between computing and telecommunications systems, which enables computers to 'talk' to each other and thus to access each other's memory banks and processing power. It is the latter, usually called information technology, which underlies the information and communication revolution of the last two decades of the twentieth century.

The first problem that needed to be addressed was to find effective means by which people and computers could communicate with each other. Almost from the beginning this was through a keyboard based on the familiar design of the typewriter, another late nineteenth-century invention which had influenced the nature of the communication process. In the earliest computers, the keystrokes made holes of predetermined patterns in strips of paper or in cards. Each letter or number was represented by a unique combination of holes. A mechanical device then 'read' this into the computer, where each combination of holes was converted into an equivalent expressed in terms of a binary number, which allowed the computer to perform its logical operations by a series of decisions between two alternatives, 'yes' and 'no'. It was a clumsy system, both time-consuming and inaccurate, in which hours of keyboarding were followed by hours of proofreading and yet more hours of tedious corrections.

For 20 years after their invention, computers were the tools of science, and largely of expensive 'big' science. They were used for vastly complex calculations in mathematics and physics, and for little else. Commercial uses were only slowly explored, the pioneers being big companies whose business involved handling large quantifies of numerical data; in practice, this meant banks, insurance companies and a few other very large corporations. Gradually, however, computing came to be used for data which was not primarily numeric. The reason for the adoption of the computer in business, industry and government, as well as in its academic applications, lay in its ability to make perfect matches between identical data, to reject all attempts to match non-identical data; and to retrieve a particular item of data with great speed from a store of almost unlimited size, as well as in its power to analyse and process data following the instructions in a program. Once data was stored in a form which the computer could read, the machine could, for example, identify all uses of a particular word, and be programmed to show that word (perhaps in some specified context) to the operator. In this way, computers could retrieve words from literary texts, or from bibliographies, and could print the context of the former or the reference for the latter. In a different application, data on individuals could be stored, analysed and retrieved to reveal, for example, information about their spending habits or other aspects of their way of life.

Conceptually, all of this was understood by the pioneers of scientific computing in the late 1940s and early 1950s; some even envisaged a time when computers would be able to 'think' *illogically*, just like a human being. Practical developments depended upon two further devices, not available until the 1970s: the transistor and the semiconductor. Transistors were developed for use in radios in the 1950s, and were the basis of the portable radios that became so common in the following decade. The properties of semiconductors, however, were investigated only in the 1960s, and it was not until ten years later that their potential was fully exploited. In essence, they facilitated the miniaturization of the memory of the computer, just as the transistor facilitated the miniaturization of its electronics. The 'microchip', made of silicon – the principal semi-conductive material used in the computing industry – contained millions of miniaturized electrical circuits, each of which held the electronically memorized program for particular sets of operations. Some of these were basic and 'simple' (the order of the letters of the Latin alphabet, for example) while others were far more complex, involving mathematical functions, or the instructions necessary to run the computer itself, such as how to translate the operator's keystrokes into images on the screen.

The same developments finally dispensed with the paper tape and punch cards of the early days of computing. Input (still from a keyboard) was directly converted into digitized form and stored on an electromagnetic disk. The disks themselves were also miniaturized, until the standard format by the late 1980s had a diameter of only 3.5 inches, on which millions of digitized characters could be stored. Programs which ran particular operations on the computer were similarly stored, and could therefore supplement the basic memory of the machine itself. The computer thus became at once a more powerful and more flexible tool; data and programs alike could be taken from machine to machine, quite apart from the ability of machines to communicate directly with each other.

Microchips were the basis of the microcomputers that came onto the market in the late 1970s; they were sold at almost unimaginably low prices, and were easy to use even for those with no scientific expertise and no real understanding of computing itself. Within a decade, the computer had become as familiar as print had been to earlier generations. Computers became smaller as they became cheaper and more powerful. The minicomputer of the 1970s, taking up a small room and presided over by specialists speaking an arcane language, was displaced by a desk-top machine no larger than a television, and, in due course, by a genuinely portable 'lap-top' computer. The image and the reality of computers were soon to be found everywhere. Machines which dispensed money appeared in the walls of banks. Clocks and watches fundamentally changed in the way in which they showed the time. Working practices changed in almost every shop, office and factory in the industrialized world. Libraries were transformed. Instant information had arrived.

Much of this information was no longer held in the memory of the computer that was used to retrieve it. Networks began to be developed for military and commercial purposes in the 1970s, and gradually became more common. The essence of a network is that digitized signals are sent from one computer, by cables or microwaves similar to those used for telephones, in a format that can be understood by another computer at the other end of the line. In this way, the user of the recipient computer can gain access to both the information and the processing power of the transmitting, or host, computer, although in practice this is often restricted by the providers of the data and the services. Networks are now commonplace. Some, especially in the academic world, are almost common-user systems like the telephone system. Others are more restricted and very expensive to use: some are private, restricted to employees of a particular company or government department; some, no doubt, are wholly secret. The great 'network of networks', the Internet, has become a familiar feature of contemporary life and, as we shall see in as become a major medium of communication.

Networks are designed primarily to provide information in 'real time', that is, the request for, and the access to, the information are immediately consecutive. The information itself is stored in a database, which is structured so that selected data can be retrieved from it. As with a book, the intellectual quality of the structure will determine the simplicity and effectiveness of the retrieval process. Because of the speed at which computers work and their ability to match like with like, searching for and retrieving information has always been one of their primary functions. In the early days of computer use in information work, the search was typically for a single term (rather like using a book index), or for a combination of terms. The latter, using a system of logic called 'Boolean algebra', was established by the mid-1970s as the normal search technique. A Boolean search allows the user to combine terms, but also to exclude other terms from the parameters of the search, using the concepts of AND, OR and NOT. These 'Boolean operators' therefore permit the construction of such requests as 'literature AND English', which will generate references to 'English literature'. How effectively a Boolean search can be conducted depends, however, on how well the database itself is constructed; in some cases, the database is so complex that the user needs to have attained an almost professional standard of skill in searching in order to make effective use of it.

The development of information retrieval as a new skill of librarians and other information workers was an important development of the 1970s and early 1980s, but the systems continued to present serious difficulties to non-expert users. The search was on for means of circumventing the complexities of Boolean methods, and, at the same time, of using ordinary language rather than complicated predetermined vocabularies of acceptable terms. A solution was found in the development of the system known as hypertext. The essence of hypertext is that it permits the user to make a series of consecutive searches without having to define a precise search term. This is achieved by building links into the database which allow the user to go from one place to the next, without any intervening steps. Thus, the user seeking information on Shakespeare may find a reference in the retrieved text to 'Globe Theatre'; if the user understands this reference, no action is taken, but if the reference is unknown, or more information is sought, a simple click on the mouse will automatically call up the relevant part of the database, from which the user can then return, at will, to the main text. This facility – electronic browsing – is fundamental to hypertext technology, and, as we shall see in Chapter 4, to the development of the World Wide Web on the Internet.

The application of the hypertext principle, is not, however, confined to textual databases. Since the mid-1980s, databases have become increasingly multimedia objects. The essence of multimedia is that it contains not merely text, but also images (still or moving) and sound (speech, music, natural sounds, and so on). All of this is digitized, and can therefore – with appropriate indexing – be searched, or be found through hypertext links. Hypermedia – the multimedia version of hypertext – is the basis of many contemporary databases, and has made the combination of words, images and sounds increasingly common for the users of information. Although the earlier audiovisual media combined the aural and the visual, they lacked the crucial element of searchability which makes digitized multimedia databases such powerful reference tools. Encyclopedias, atlases and similar works of reference, as well as highly specialized training tools in fields as diverse as engineering and surgery, are increasingly published in multimedia rather than printed or audiovisual formats.

The normal physical format for multimedia objects is the optical disc, familiar as the compact disc or CD. The CD is now a commonplace object. It first came into general use as a medium for recorded sound of extraordinarily high quality, and has indeed largely displaced the earlier recorded sound formats such as magnetic tape and vinyl records. An optical disc, however, can be used for any digitized data. The data on the audio CD is retrieved by a sound system, which translates it into audio signals played through amplifiers and loudspeakers. In exactly the same way, the digitized data in a textual database can be retrieved through a computer system and displayed on a screen. This has been developed commercially as the CD-ROM (compact disc –

read only memory), which is now familiar in almost all libraries and a growing number of businesses and homes. The CD-ROM need not be solely textual. Multimedia CD-ROMs are increasingly common, for it is they that provide the format for the electronic works of reference. The combination of CD-ROM and hypermedia is a powerful one; indeed, it is probably the most powerful information retrieval tool that has ever been made available to all but a handful of professional users. A CD-ROM drive is now a normal feature of desk-top and lap-top computers, as the format has become a standard tool of information retrieval.

The effects of the digital revolution are, however, being felt far beyond the narrow confines of the world of information storage and retrieval. The audio CD is merely one example of the transformative consequences of the technology. Conventional communications systems have also been changed almost beyond recognition. The telephone, the Victorian device which created the telecommunications industry, has been one of the greatest beneficiaries. A wide range of services are now offered by telecommunications companies themselves, often in competition with one another, quite apart from the almost limitless services that can be obtained over the telephone from banking, through mail order shopping to entertainment services of varying degrees of social acceptability. Digital exchanges have replaced the old electromechanical devices, and direct dialling across the world is commonplace. We can make calls using credit cards and charge cards, store and retrieve numbers and make use of a dozen other systems that were unknown a decade ago. The touch-tone telephone makes all this possible by digitizing the tones and transmitting them as messages to computers.

Perhaps the greatest revolution in personal telecommunications has been the mobile phone. This too is a child of the digital revolution both in its hardware and in the networks. If the mobile phone is not always regarded as an unmixed blessing, it is nevertheless the case that it has become essential to the private and

professional lives of millions of people across the globe. T
nology for accessing the Internet from a mobile phone ___ ____y
exists; the portable battery-operated lap-top and the mobile
phone together will finally free us from the office or indeed any
other fixed location for communicating with the rest of the world.
The impact of this next phase of the digital revolution on our
habits of work and leisure can already be imagined, and will soon
be realized.

Meanwhile, the mass media are also being changed by digitization. Digital radio and television, about to be introduced into
Britain, will bring a higher technical quality of reception than has
ever been possible before, and at the same time open up the possibility of dozens, perhaps hundreds, of new channels. Again, this
may not be seen as an unmixed blessing, but as the technologies
become more common and the cost of acquiring and using them
falls, the prospect of truly community-based broadcasting becomes
more real, leading to radically wider access to television, the most
powerful of the mass media.

An image of instantaneous worldwide access to information
would, however, be somewhat deceptive. Behind the third revolution lies an industry even more capital intensive, and even more
competitive, than those of the first and second. Instant information is indeed available if the owners of the information would
make it so, and if the seekers were able to gain access to it. The
vast costs of installing computer systems are inevitably passed on
to the customers of millions of businesses. There is human cost in
the retraining of staff (not always successfully) to use the new
technology. The new industry, either directly or indirectly, has
absorbed much of the surplus capital in western countries.
Moreover, some of the promises have failed. Even in the 1990s,
not all computers, and certainly not all software, are reliable,
idiot-proof and user-friendly, even when allegedly designed for
non-expert users. Instant information is indeed available to the
money dealer or the stockbroker – at a very high cost – but infor-

mation systems for the domestic market have so far been only a limited success. Some of the democratizing effects of the first two revolutions in communications and information are even apparently in danger of being reversed in the third. Access to information is increasingly dependent on wealth and skills to an extent that has not been true in the world of print since the nineteenth century, nor in the mass media for most of their existence.

That is the paradox. Technology has made more information more available to more people than at any time in tens of thousands of years of human history. But the same technology has made access to it more difficult. It is that paradox, and some of its implications, which subsequent chapters seek to explore.

3

THE ECONOMIC DIMENSION
| The information market-place

THE PUBLISHING INDUSTRY:
A PARADIGM OF INFORMATION TRANSFER

The mechanisms that have been developed for the transfer of information from source to user all require significant capital investment. The role of information in society can only be properly understood in a context in which its cost and monetary value are properly taken into account. Recent developments in information technology, and the gradual convergence of previously separate technologies, have tended to emphasize both the cost of the infrastructure of information systems and that of delivering the service to the user. The change, however, has been one of degree rather than of kind. As we saw in Chapter 1, ever since the invention of printing, and in a very limited way even before that, there has been an overtly commercial element in the information transfer process. The trade in the printed word is perhaps not the only comparison which could be used as a model for the commercialization of computer-based information service provision, but it is certainly the most familiar. There is a good reason for this: print, in all its manifestations, is still the most common, and remains the most important,information medium in terms of the quantity of stored information which is uniquely available. It is, therefore, with print that we shall begin.

The publishing industry – the producer of books, magazines and newspapers – is merely one part of a larger complex of trades and industries. The size and scale of the operation of individual firms within this complex varies from vast multinational corporations, such as News International, at one extreme, to, at the other, a small bookshop owned and operated by a single person. Linking these improbable partners is a long chain of supply which provides the route along which information can travel from source to user. Inevitably, however, the chain is distorted by commercial pressures, and the free flow of information itself may sometimes be disrupted by accident or design. In other words, the financial parameters within which publishing (like all the other sectors of the information industry) must work, acts as both an accelerator and a brake in the process of information supply.

The literal meaning of the verb 'to publish' is 'to make public', but in common usage it has taken on the more familiar sense of 'to issue copies of a book, magazine, newspaper, etc., for sale'. Although this is the only sensible way in which to use the word, it is important to remember its root meaning. At the heart of the publishing process lies the concept of *dissemination*. In the publishing industry, this means the dissemination of information which has been put into a material form, normally print on paper. It is the process of translating the information into this material form which determines the nature of the publishing industry itself.

AUTHORS AND PUBLISHERS

A publisher is essentially an intermediary between author and reader. The process of knowledge creation and information dissemination begins, therefore, with the author. The 'author', however, is a concept as multifaceted as the 'publisher'. The classic model is of the individual using knowledge or imagination to create a text which in some way expresses what the author wishes to convey to the reader. It is a model derived essentially from the 'creative' writer, the poet or novelist, although it can certainly be applied to the authors of certain kinds of non-fiction as well. Few texts, however, are created wholly out of the imagination of the author.[1] Many novelists undertake research; this may involve the study of subjects as diverse as social history or aircraft design depending on the subject matter of the book. Even where no formal research is undertaken, novelists are typically drawing on knowledge acquired by experience as well as relying on pure invention. The imaginative element often lies in the use made of knowledge, whether or not its acquisition is experiential.

As we move further away from fiction, the authorial model gradually changes. A work of non-fiction can be written in a way which is not unlike writing a novel. An individual author researches a topic, analyses the material, reduces it to a logical and often narrative form, and composes the work. Indeed, this is the classic model of scholarship in the humanities and much of the writing of commercial non-fiction of the sort seen in bookshops and public libraries. Methods may vary between individual authors, partly because of their own habits and preferences, and partly because of the nature of their subjects and the sources of information which they use, but the variations are less important than the fundamental similarities.

In these two models, which represent the common understanding of how books are written, the commercial element may, at first sight, seem to be lacking. This is not the case, for the author must find someone who is willing to take the risk of turning the created work into a form in which it can be distributed. Since

---

[1] I am conscious of using words such as 'author' and 'text' which are the subject of much controversy among literary critics and theorists. These theories are interesting and important but are not my immediate concern here. I am using the words in their common and widely understood meanings in which the 'author' is the person (or as we shall see persons) responsible for the creation of the 'text' which is in turn simply taken to mean that which is created by the author. The circularity of this argument does not deter me; for the present purpose commonly understood significations are more important than theoretical niceties. Some variations on even this 'simple' meaning of 'author' are however considered in the following paragraphs.

authors are typically aiming at printed publication in the form of
a book, that intermediary is the publisher, and it is to the publisher that the author sells the work. For some authors, the
money received for that sale may be a minor consideration, but
for many it predominates. The popular novelist is essentially the
producer of a highly profitable commodity. The commodity may
have some cultural or literary value, if only as a socially acceptable form of entertainment, but it is nevertheless a commodity.
The author may even enjoy the process of creating the commodity – the evidence is that most authors do – but that does not in
itself change the perception of the activity as being·principally
commercial. The same is true of almost all non-fiction; indeed,
the vast majority of such books are commissioned by publishers
from authors, so that, at the time of writing, the author knows
that the product, provided that it meets the publisher's expectations, will indeed be sold.

It might be argued that there is another model, in which the
author of a work of literature or scholarship writes without
thought of financial gain. There are indeed such authors, but
even they are writing in the hope of being read because they
believe they have something to say. It is also possible for authors
to circumvent conventional channels of publication and distribution, but in so doing they limit their audience and their impact.
In practice, to reach even the limited readership which is normal
for a literary novel or a scholarly monograph, authors are obliged
to use commercial publication mechanisms. This may bring a
coincidental, although very small, financial reward; it may bring
other rewards to which the author attaches a higher value, in
terms of fame or employment. But the financial implications are
everywhere; we have created a chain of information supply in
which the dissemination of the printed word can be achieved
only by the exchange of money.

The commercial dimension is even more overt when we move
away from the 'simple' historical model of authorship. The author

of a work of non-fiction may be helped by others who work as research assistants; the public acknowledgement of their roles can vary from a brief mention in a preface to a statement of joint authorship on the title-page. In the academic world a whole series of conventions and courtesies (which differ somewhat between disciplines) surround such matters; for other writers of non-fiction they are determined by personal inclination or contractual agreement. At one end of the scale is the paid researcher who provides the information from which the author fashions the book, and may be fully acknowledged as a joint or even coequal author; at the other is the ghost writer who actually writes the book but whose identity and existence may be wholly concealed from the reader. The concept of 'author' is far less easily defined when two or more people are the creators of a particular work, differing both in their inputs and in the public acknowledgement of their respective contributions.

As the group of contributors to authoring a work becomes larger, their relationships become more complex. The role of the publisher as financier of the operation then becomes even more important. Authors do not generally employ assistants or ghosts to work on books with them or for them unless publication is contractually guaranteed; in that case, the costs are effectively borne by the publisher. Where a work is avowedly of multiple authorship, the centrality of the publisher's role is even more apparent. A volume of essays on a particular topic, for example, will typically be commissioned by a publisher from an editor. It is the editor's job to recruit a team of contributors, all of whom, however, are directly contracted to the publisher by whom they are paid. The editor's input is primarily intellectual, while the publisher's role is principally commercial. In more complex cases, such as a major encyclopedia, the editorial role may be undertaken by a team of people, perhaps with a body of advisers, and with a large number of contributors. The operation then has a major administrative dimension as well as an intellectual one.

These simple and familiar examples illustrate the variety and complexity of the publishing process even in its most basic relationship, that of the author and publisher of a book. If we look beyond books to newspapers and magazines, we find yet another set of relationships. Both of these forms of periodical have editors who normally have the authority to decide what shall be printed and what shall not. The authors, however, are journalists who, in many cases, are direct employees of the publishing house which owns the title. They are told what to write about, either generally (as in being employed as a political correspondent) or specifically (as in being sent to interview a particular person). What they write may be modified, often quite drastically, by the editor, or by sub-editors employed for that very purpose. These changes depersonalize the writing process. The nineteenth-century convention of the anonymity of journalists (which survived until after World War II on some newspapers and magazines) was rooted in a realistic recognition of this relationship. The story 'by' a particular journalist is often merely based on that journalist's reports. These are edited for length, style and content by a sub-editor and perhaps again by the editor; they are introduced by a headline also written by the sub-editor or editor, which may itself give a particular bias to the reader's perception of the story. The journalist's original version may even be augmented by additional information from other sources. Not all journalists, or indeed editors, work in this way. Some are self-employed, and, like some writers of books, are commissioned to write particular articles on specific topics, or perhaps to contribute a regular feature or column. Editorial control is still there, but the relationship is perhaps a more equal one.

Even the most cursory consideration of how writers work in the newspaper and magazine industries reveals very starkly the commercial basis of the author–publisher relationship, and consequently the importance of that commercial relationship in the process of information transfer. The great variety of forms of

printed publication means that there are many different manifestations of this relationship, but there is, on closer analysis, little
fundamental difference between them. An author who wants to
communicate with a reader can only do so if there is a publisher
willing and able to facilitate this. At the heart of the creative
process of writing lies a commercial transaction without which
the results of the author's creativity cannot be shared with an
audience.

The role of the publisher is central in the information market
place because it is the publisher whose risk capital allows it to
operate. In book publishing, the editor is the *de facto* gatekeeper
at the entrance to the market. The publisher's editor has a very
different role from the newspaper editor, although they are both
employed by the publisher to act as arbiters of what is produced
in the publisher's name. The primary role of the publisher's editor
is to select material for publication, although this process is by no
means as passive as that statement might imply. Again, a simple
model is a useful starting-point. In such a model, an author writes
a book and sends it speculatively to a publisher, it is read by an
editor, accepted and published. That model might itself be an
interesting subject for a novel for it is indeed little more than a
work of fiction. A very few books, mainly first novels, do reach
print in this way. Publishers are bombarded with such works from
unknown authors. Some of them are read; a very few (estimates
hover at around 1% of those submitted) are accepted and published. It is one way to break into print, but it is neither the most
common nor the most effective.

Most writers of books have previous experience as writers,
whether as journalists, magazine contributors or academics.
Virtually all non-fiction is commissioned from an author before it
is written, on the basis of a synopsis which is often developed
jointly between author and editor. Many authors, and probably
all who depend on writing as their main source of income, use literary agents to negotiate with publishers and others on their

behalf. The author who knows that the book will be published has to work within the constraints of the market-place in fulfilling a contractual obligation to the publisher. These constraints are manifold. A typical contract specifies the subject of the book (usually in the form of a working title), its approximate length, when it is to be delivered to the publisher and in what form. In return the author normally receives a sum of money on signature of contract, and a further sum on delivery and acceptance of the work; thereafter, he or she is paid a percentage (usually between 10% and 12.5%) of the receipts from the sale of the book, known as a royalty.

The contract is itself determined by the operation of the information market-place. The subject, and perhaps the author, of the book is its principal selling point, and the publisher's willingness to take on a particular title rests ultimately on an estimate of its marketability. There are some data which can be used as a guide. Typically, about 10% of the annual output of British publishers is of works of fiction and a further 8% or 9% consists of children's books; the remaining 80% or so is spread across the whole range of non-fiction. History and biography are by far the most popular categories, with science, medicine, sociology, business books and computing not far behind, but none of these account for more than 5% of the output, and typically they are between 3% and 4%. This is critical to the book publisher's understanding of the information market-place: it is very diverse.

THE DIVERSITY OF PUBLISHING

Few publishers try to work across the whole range of subjects and levels of books. In the larger companies which, as we shall see, now typify the publishing industry, specialist editors are normally responsible for different parts of the list. The basic division is between fiction and non-fiction, although both of these are usually further subdivided. In trade jargon, fiction is divided between 'literary' and 'popular', although even fiction editors sometimes have difficulty in explaining the difference between them. The implication is that it is qualitative. A cynical, but not entirely unrealistic, definition might be to regard popular fiction as fiction which sells and literary fiction as fiction which does not; but this is too crude, and disguises genuine differences. Under the 'popular' umbrella there are many different genres, often used by publishers, librarians and readers to define their own interests; these are such categories as 'science fiction', 'thrillers', 'romances', 'historical novels', and so on.

Non-fiction is, perhaps surprisingly, even less easy to categorize. Many publishing houses specialize in particular subject areas, such as law, medicine or business books. Others cover a wider range, and it is in such firms that specialist editors are typically employed. A distinction which is normally made is between non-fiction for the specialist and non-fiction for the general reader, although there is some overlap. The former is usually known as 'academic' or 'STM' (scientific–technical–medical) publishing, and the latter as 'trade' or 'general trade' non-fiction. These distinctions are essentially market-driven. Academic or STM books are aimed at a small but easily definable market. It is international, especially for books written in English, and it is very largely institutional. Trade non-fiction, on the other hand, is intended to have a wider appeal: it is more often seen in bookshops (although the library market is still of great importance), reviewed in newspapers, recorded in bestseller lists and, in some cases, reprinted in paperback. An author's ability to reach the right audience is effectively determined by the right choice of publisher, and the publisher's understanding of the market for that particular book. That, in turn, depends on the editor.

The precise nature of the editorial role in a publishing house varies according to what is being published, and perhaps the traditions and customs of the firm, but any good editor is an active participant in the publishing process. Above all, the editor is a recruiter of authors, often from among those whose reputation has been established in other ways. The pool for non-fiction includes journalists and other professional writers, as well as academics. It is an essential part of editors' jobs to keep abreast of the fields with which they are concerned. This is done partly through market research, usually in the form of statistical data published regularly by the Publishers' Association, various official and semi-official agencies such as the Central Statistical Office and the Library and Information Statistics Unit, trade journals such as *The Bookseller* and *Publishers' Weekly*, and independent market surveys such as those in *Euromonitor*. Even more important, however, is the development and exploitation of a network of contacts built up over many years in the trade, in the literary and academic worlds and among journalists and other opinion-makers. This is the invisible college of publishing; a working knowledge of it is the core of the editor's expertise. This knowledge is a valuable if ill-defined commodity, which editors can take from job to job, sometimes complete with the authors whose careers they have helped to develop.

The importance of the editorial role becomes greater when the end-product is more complex. For a multi-authored work, or for major works of reference, the publishing house is a party to many different contractual obligations, all of which have to be brought to fruition at the right moment and in the right order if the book is to be successful. The publisher's editor and the authors or editors of such works collaborate closely as a team, further diluting the concept of authors and publishers as separate and even conflicting entities

The editor's job does not end when the book is written. Before the book can reach the bookshops it needs to go through a whole series of operations. Traditionally, the work was read by an expert in the field, or a person of literary judgement, before it was finally accepted. This form of quality control, however, is not as stringent as it used to be. The sheer quantity of material which crosses an editor's desk, and the need to work quickly in order to maximize the immediate financial returns on a book, have partly eliminated it. So too has modern technology. When an author submits work on a disk, as is now usually the case, the temptation to treat that as an authoritative file (as well as the potential technical problems of editing it) is often too strong to resist. Above all, however, there are financial pressures on the editor. A publisher gets no return on the investment in a title until it is in the bookshops; from receipt of text from the author to the first sales rarely takes less than six months. During all of that time, the publisher is spending more money: the author has already been partly paid; editors have to be paid; the book has to be printed and bound; and most of the costs of advertising and marketing are incurred. Speed is paramount, for large and small publishers alike, so that the book is to begin to earn its living.

The concern of the editor, therefore, is to put the book into a saleable form as quickly as possible. It is edited, for style and spelling if not for content, designed and then sent for typesetting. This may be from disks supplied by the author, but if the text has to be keyboarded again for some reason, it will have to be proofread once each by the typesetter (although this is increasingly unusual) and by the publisher, and normally by the author as well. In any case, authors expect to see proofs, and indeed there may be some additional work to do at this stage, such as the compilation of an index. While all of this is going on, the book is advertised through the trade press, or, in some cases, by direct mailshots to potential customers on the publisher's mailing list, or the mailing list of agencies which the publisher uses. Eventually, when the book is printed, it goes to a warehouse from which it will be distributed either by the publishers themselves, or by a distribution agency whom they employ. Thirty days after the first copy is sold to a bookseller, the publisher will, at last, get some revenue to set against the very substantial investment which has been made.

This chain of communication from author to reader is informed and determined at every stage by commercial considerations. Quality is important, and few publishers would consciously produce an inferior product. There are, however, no absolute criteria of quality. Novels which would, on literary grounds, be wholly unacceptable to one publisher, are the mainstay of another; nonfiction which would not see the light of day from a university press may top the bestseller lists for weeks and be the pride and joy of a general trade publisher. The industry is large enough to be diverse; in this diversity lies both its strength and its weakness.

NEW DIRECTIONS IN PUBLISHING

The contemporary practices of traditional publishing have been dealt with at some length because the book publishing process has become the paradigm of information transfer. Even its vocabulary has been carried into new technologies, where there is no hesitation in talking about the 'publication' of educational videos or computer software, and indeed some of these products are sold through 'bookshops'. The convergence of technologies, and the gradual displacement of print by other media, has further confused the issue. Databases, held by their creators and accessible online through networks and hosts, are, in the most literal sense 'published', that is they are made public. Many, however, are by no means in the public domain in the same way that books are, because the commercial basis on which access is achieved is quite different. Buying access to a database, which normally involves purchasing both time and information, is a very different commercial transaction from buying a book. In a library, a reference book bought by the institution instantly becomes a multiuser tool; an online search of a distant database, on the other hand, is conducted by or, more often, for an individual user, and can be precisely costed and therefore accurately charged. Although the intellectual processes and editorial procedures in the compilation of a database are, both conceptually and in many functional aspects, analogous to the compilation of a conventional printed reference book, the methods and circumstances of access to the end-product are fundamentally different. The implications of these differences will be explored in greater detail in Chapter 4.

The use of information technology has, however, also resulted in profound changes in the world of publishing and printed information, as was suggested in Chapter 2. This manifests itself in many ways. Even within the conventional publishing process, as it has been described, the use of computers has put the author in a more powerful and perhaps more responsible position, *vis-à-vis* the editor. The demand for text to be submitted in electronic form has shifted some aspects of publishing away from the publisher. The concept of 'house style', by which publishers traditionally imposed their own practices of italicization, indentation and other technical features on the text, becomes suddenly less attractive when it involves lengthy and expensive editing of a text which is already internally consistent when it arrives from the author, even if it does not precisely conform to the publisher's own absolute preferences. This is one of those technological paradoxes referred to at the end of Chapter 2; electronic text is in many ways easier to manipulate than text on paper, but the potential problems of doing so often deter the editor from intervening.

Changes in editorial practices, by no means all of them intentional, are not the only way in which computers have impinged on publishing. Quite apart from straightforward business uses such as are now found in almost all organizations, computers are used throughout the printing industry, where they have displaced traditional typesetting methods (and also control much of the printing machinery) and are integral to book ordering and distribution systems in most industrialized countries. Bibliographic databases, often compiled at national level, are as important in the book trade as they are to librarians, and the International

Standard Book Number (ISBN) and its associated bar-code is used as a unique identifier of a book as much in the trade as it is in libraries.

These changes have been important; after 20 years of experimentation, and not a few failures, the perspective is now long enough for us to see that the use of computers has probably been a factor in holding book prices at a reasonable level and keeping the increases in prices roughly in line with the general rate of price inflation. Even more important changes, however, are taking place in those areas of the market where information technology has done more than merely change the means by which books are written, edited, printed and distributed. In some fields of publishing, the use of computers has facilitated wholly new developments whose products have begun to displace the printed book itself. These developments have involved the creation of information media which, while retaining much of the ease of use of the book, can also overcome some of its inherent disadvantages The printed book is, in many ways, a remarkably flexible medium. It is portable, easily stored, familiar, user- friendly and adaptable to many purposes. It does, however, have two major limitations: it is impossible to change, and it can only be consulted in an essentially linear mode. Both of these points deserve further explanation.

Once a book has been printed, it cannot be altered except by reprinting from a new, or amended, setting of the type or its computer-generated equivalent. This process is both time-consuming and expensive, and runs up against the basic economics of book production. Typically, books are printed in editions ('print runs' in the normal trade parlance) of between a few hundred and many tens of thousands, but most often between 1500 and 5000 copies. This gives access to some of the economies of scale which characterize mass production processes in other industries, but by no means to all of them. The inhibitory factor lies in the size, or rather the smallness, of the print run itself. A modern printing press can print 1500 copies of a sheet in far less than one hour; a typical book contains no more than between 10 and 15 sheets, each folded to make 16 or 32 pages. In theory then, a print run of 1500 copies of a book can be completed in a working day. In practice, however, the whole process is delayed by what happens between sheets, when the metal plate from which the printed impression is actually made has to be removed from the press and the plate for the next sheet substituted for it. This downtime (known traditionally as 'make-ready' time) adds significantly to the delays and costs of printing. The shorter the print run, the larger the proportion of down time during the printing process, inevitably increasing the costs.

Because of this basic technological consideration, print runs of less than about 500 are almost never economic using traditional, non-digital printing, and even that is acceptable only for specialized books where the market will bear a consequently high price although future technical developments may enable even this obstacle to be overcome. At present, if a book becomes out of date, it can only be updated if it is printed in similar numbers. Sometimes this happens; there are obvious examples of books which are updated at regular intervals (such as *Who's Who* or *Wisden's Cricketers' Almanac*, for example) and of others (such as this one) which are updated at irregular intervals as the need arises. Economically, however, this can only be justified if the market for the new edition is comparable with that for the old one; hence revised editions of annuals or reprints of textbooks used by successive generations of students are economically viable, but for most books they are not. As a result, books are now typically 'in print' (that is available through normal commercial channels) for little more than a year or so, at which point it often makes more sense for a publisher to replace the title by a new one on a similar subject rather than revise an existing title for which most of the market potential has been exhausted. This, however, involves, substantial reinvestment. The inflexibility of the text of a printed book, and the need to produce the book itself in substantial quantities, are the major disadvantages of the medium, and never more so than at a time when the quantity of information is increasing, and demand for its currency is insistent.

The second inhibitory factor is inherent in the codex form of the book itself: it is linear. It is, of course, possible to turn to any given page of a book without starting at page 1 and working forward from there. It is indeed the normal practice in almost all non-fiction to provide tables of contents and indexes which are designed to facilitate precisely that method of use. On the other hand, the user is limited in two important ways. First, it is not possible to consult more than one page at the same time, or to bring together information from more than one page, without transferring it to some other medium by taking notes or making photocopies, for example. Secondly, the use of the various searching devices such as an index is limited by the work of their compilers; the index leads only to the passages chosen by the indexer, even if, in practice, the indexing terms themselves may not represent the interests of a particular user. It is in this sense that the linear nature of the book, inherent in its physical form, makes it so unsatisfactory for some purposes.

THE IMPACT OF COMPUTERS

For over 500 years, these limitations were accepted; at first, perhaps this was because the printed book represented such a great advance on its manuscript predecessor, and later simply because of familiarity and inertia. With computers, however, the limitations no longer exist. First, the updating, revision and correction of data can be a continuous process, and the user can have virtually instantaneous access to the updated version. This is precisely what happens in a computerized library catalogue, where the entries for new books can be immediately incorporated into the file, without any delays for filing cards or pasting slips into guard books. For the user of a library catalogue, the decrease in delay is convenient; for the user of a financial information service, continuous updating and absolute currency of information is essential. The computer thus overcomes the first of the great limitations of print because it can actually exploit the essential impermanence of an electronic information store.

The consultation of the data in that store is not confined by the linear characteristics of the book. A search, making use of an indexing term which is under the effective control of the user, will reveal all uses of the term in the store, and will bring them together on the screen or on successive screens from which they can then, if the user so wishes, be printed out. The search is controlled by the user, not by the indexer. Once the data has been retrieved, it can be processed in many different ways. It may merely be printed, so that it can be filed like a printed document or a photocopy. It can, however, be downloaded into other files, combined with data from other sources, and electronically processed in a way devised by the user. The possibilities are almost limitless.

For some years, the obvious theoretical benefits of computer-held files as against printed books were not fully or adequately exploited. There were some technical reasons for this, as well as inevitable and natural human resistance to change. It was, however, the economic factors which were the greatest inhibitors of change. The money broker does indeed need instant access to information; research scientists, on the other hand, do not, even though they want to minimize the delay. It is no accident that the earliest commercially successful databases were in such fields as finance and law, where it is commercially important to have current and accurate information. The cost of instant access to information was very high in the 1970s and early 1980s, even though the technology for it existed. Typically, it was achieved through telecommunications links to host computers in which databases were held.

Both the information itself and the use of the communications systems were valorized. There has been a good deal of debate about the valorization of information and the partial commodification of information services which it has brought in its wake. The charge for access included both the cost of the information (determined and assigned by the creators and owners of the database) and the cost of the telecommunications (determined by the service provider). It is important to distinguish between the various elements which comprise this charge and form the basis of the commercial transaction. The products of the information industry have been in the commercial domain for over 500 years. In general, however, the price of the product has related to its material production, with the cost of its intellectual content a comparatively less important issue. Typically, no more than about 10% of the total revenue accrued to the creator of the intellectual content, usually an author. The rest of the price represented a return (intended to be profitable) on the publisher's investment in editorial time, business infrastructure, materials and production. When information is taken from databases rather than a printed source, however, it is possible to make a direct charge for each consultation. The system itself can record the identity of the user, the information sought and obtained and the timespan of the search. Charges may accrue for communications time, and for the data retrieved. In other words, commodification has been extended from the product to its contents and the means of accessing its contents.

This is a critical shift in the structure of the information market place. The printed book was essentially a common-user item, a good acquired by purchase and thereafter available freely to all who had access to it. Historically, where such access has been through libraries, it has been uncharged at the point and time of consultation. Accessing a database is quite different. The information intermediary does not acquire the database itself, but the right to use it; this is true whether consultation is online or on some offline medium such as CD-ROM. The creator and owner of the database cannot, therefore, recoup the costs of compilation and production by the sale of a product. What is sold is a service. The charge derives from the value which is added to the information, from the perspective of the end-user, by the way in which it has been collected, sorted, analysed and presented. The value-added element is new, and fundamentally different from the traditional charge for an information product. The charge, like the information which is provided, is tailored to the precise needs of the recipient. This concept is explored in more detail in Chapter 5.

Long and complex searches attract very high communications costs, especially for European users, who are often searching databases held in the USA and working from countries where the cost of telecommunications is itself high by American standards. Some of the theoretical advantages of online searching of databases could not be fully exploited because it was economically necessary to use skilled intermediaries (usually librarians) in order to minimize the cost. End-users were thus distanced from the information-seeking process, and that process was not fully informed by their specialist subject knowledge. Out of this, there developed a new branch of the information profession itself, in which brokers operated on behalf of clients, searching databases to meet their information needs, providing either on-demand services or a continuous service of provision of relevant information. The brokerage was another value-added element in the transaction, and perhaps completed the absorption of certain kinds of information provision into the sphere of commerce.

Online databases starkly illuminated the financial dimension of the information market-place. The demand was there, but many potential customers did not have sufficient resources to buy the product. Inevitably, a new product was developed which would bring supply and demand into balance within the financial limitations of the customers. This product was the CD-ROM, which has all the advantages, except one, of the online database: it can be searched freely, downloaded without difficulty, and, with appropriate software, is easy to use even for the untrained or inexperienced user. What it lacks is currency, for a CD-ROM, like a book, cannot be updated once it has been made. On the other hand, the files which are reproduced on it can, and because the actual process of producing the disc is both cheap and simple (and is economic in far shorter 'print runs' than is the case with traditionally printed books), a new disc can be produced at regular intervals (usually of between three and twelve months) to ensure that, for all practical purposes, the database is as current as most ordinary users will ever need. Whatever disadvantages this may entail are more than counterbalanced by the fact that there are no charges for access, because, like a book, once the initial purchase has been made, the disc can be used by an unlimited number of users and an unlimited number of times, although the publisher retains control of the data, and CD-ROMs can be used in libraries only under licence agreements. Ironically, consultation often takes place over a network (subject to the conditions of the licensing arrangements), so that CD-ROM itself has become an online medium. Indeed, the distinction between online and CD-ROM access to a database is increasingly meaningless. Both are merely tools which enable the user to find the information; the decision on which to use is essentially financial rather than technical, so that databases in heavy use in comparatively badly funded sectors, like academic research, tend to be on CD-ROM, since absolute currency is less important than cost. Only in sectors such as financial services and the money markets, where absolute currency is essential, will online access continue to be economically viable.

It is no surprise that CD-ROM has been such a success, or that it has probably made more inroads into the market for printed books than any previous computer-based information medium. There are significant areas of reference book publishing in which

CD-ROM has all but displaced the printed word; these include indexes, annual bibliographies and many abstracts, some of which were previously available online, and some only in printed form. CD-ROM is the ideal compromise, for it does well what the printed book does badly, and it does cheaply what an online system does expensively.

The still brief history (but probably long future) of CD-ROM has brought the publishing industry closer than ever to the information technology industry. Competition has been inevitable, but so has cooperation, for publishers themselves recognize the need to adapt to new and more economic technologies that users actually want. Indeed, unlike many previous non-book formats, the CD-ROM market is largely dominated by familiar names from the publishing world, for their editorial expertise and market experience can be directly translated from the older to the newer medium.

THE INTERDEPENDENT MEDIA: CONVERGENCE AND CHANGE

Technological developments and economic necessity have been the driving forces behind important changes in the chain of information transfer from author to reader, or from creator to user. Some traditional media have been changed; others have been wholly or partly displaced. The result is greater diversity, in which the wider range of choice allows the producer and the user to determine the most suitable medium for a particular purpose. CD-ROM is not successful simply because it works; it is successful because customers find it useful, and it can do things for them that they want, at prices that they (or their information providers) can afford. This is not the only way in which consumer choice has determined how information media have changed. An equally striking and more generally applicable example is to be found in the newspaper industry.

Throughout the industrialized world, most people now obtain whatever knowledge they have of current affairs from television and radio. Almost all broadcasting services have news bulletins of some sort (there are exceptions among the more specialized satellite and cable services), and most make use of either correspondents or agencies which allow them to give virtually instantaneous access to the news as it breaks. News channels, such as Cable News Network (CNN), have, despite gloomy forecasts, proved to be a great success, and the demand for such channels, both on radio and on television, appears to be a real one. There is no doubt that the interest in the news is both widespread and genuine. At the same time, the circulation of newspapers has fallen dramatically during the last 30 years. Again, we do not have to look far for the reason. Broadcast news is both easier to absorb and cheaper to receive than printed news. The demise of the newspaper has been forecast more than once, and, indeed, many newspapers have closed; yet many remain, and many of them are very successful.

The survival of the newspaper as a mass medium has been achieved by adaptation to changed circumstances. In Britain, this evolutionary development has had two dimensions. At one end of the market, the 'serious' press has increasingly taken on the characteristics of a news magazine. Although there is still much reporting of 'hard' news in the British broadsheets, there is also a great deal of comment, interpretation, analysis and background, as well as features on a wide range of topics from science to fashion. At the other (and more profitable) end of the market, news reporting in the traditional sense has almost vanished; politics is dealt with largely at the level of abuse, personal interest stories and covert or overt commentary, while much of the 'news' is actually about such matters as television soap operas (and their stars), the private lives of famous people, and the like.

In fact, both the broadsheets and the tabloids are doing the same thing, and working from similar assumptions: they are finding ways to survive as *news*papers in a society in which they are not the preferred *news* medium. They have done so by changing the definition of news. Much of what is written in them actually assumes a basic factual knowledge of persons and events, knowledge which has been acquired through the broadcast media. Because they cannot compete in immediacy, they compete in depth and in detail; they report what radio and television cannot report because of the time limitations on their broadcasts. This has had further consequences. The changes in the broadsheet newspapers have been a factor in driving some British weeklies out of business, for the newspapers now perform the function formerly unique to them, and indeed in preventing the development of American-style news magazines (such as *Time* and *Newsweek*) in Britain, because they already fulfil much of their potential role. The tabloids have had a similar effect on different magazines. In other words, the news market, like the very different market for abstracts of papers in scientific journals, has been changed under consumer pressure. Consumers turn to the broadcast media for instant news, and to the print media for analysis, detail and diversity. The survival of the newspaper has been made possible by the publishers' recognition of the changed circumstances in the information market-place.

The interrelated and interdependent roles of different media and technologies are being redefined by economic and cultural factors, and the perceptions and wishes of their customers and audiences. The market-place is both growing and fragmenting. Technologies as well as suppliers are in competition with each other, and there is only limited space for successful operations. The changing nature of newspapers and the rise of the CD-ROM are only two examples of the results of this process. Underlying all of this change is the changing structure of the communications industry, which, like its technology, is increasingly global rather than national, with all the implications of such universality for the countries in which it operates. Even a so comparatively parochial dimension of the industry as British publishing illustrates this point.

The UK book market was worth some £2.8 million in 1994, a figure roughly in line with the immediately preceding years. This market was dominated by four major groups, each of them embracing a wide range of activities in both book publishing and other media. All of them had a significant presence in the other major (and indeed far larger) English-language market, the USA, and all were also involved in other media.

The largest general trade publisher in Britain was Random Century, an American publishing company which is an amalgamation of the long-established New York firm of Random House with the Anglo-American consortium of Century-Hutchinson. Its British imprints are some of the best known in the trade; they include some widely respected 'quality' publishers, including Bodley Head, Jonathan Cape and Chatto & Windus. The company is also heavily involved, through some of its other imprints, in academic and STM publishing, and in publishing educational books. Random Century, however, is still largely a publishing conglomerate.

HarperCollins, the second of these four major groups, has moved far beyond that, and has tentacles across the media throughout the world. It was formed in the early 1980s, when Rupert Murdoch, the Australian media magnate, took over two prestigious but ailing publishing houses, Harper & Row in the USA, and Collins in Britain. They were different but complementary. Harper & Row was an academic and professional publisher, with a long history of respectability in that field. Collins was no less respectable, but had built its reputation on middlebrow fiction, popular religious books and the semi-popular non-fiction in its Fontana list. It was a good combination, but under the Murdoch umbrella HarperCollins is really the book publishing arm of News International, whose interests include *The Times*, *The Sun* and *The Sunday Times*, as well as Australian papers and the *New York Daily News*. Murdoch's other involvements in the communications industry include BSkyB, the only significant satellite broadcaster in the UK market. The various parts of HarperCollins have been able to defend their editorial independence under this regime, but they are inevitably subjected to more stringent financial disciplines. Being a part of one of the world's largest companies is very different from being a small or historic family publishing house.

It is, however, with two other companies that we reach the multimedia heart of the industry. Reed International, whose book publishing alone turned over some £120 million in 1994, was formed in the 1970s, and now includes a whole range of British and foreign publishers. These include Heinemann, Methuen, Philip and Octopus in Britain, R. R. Bowker in the USA, K. G. Saur in Germany, and other interests in Australia. This, however, is only the beginning of an account of Reed's interests, which include magazines, British regional newspapers, scholarly and scientific journals, satellite broadcasting, online information services and CD-ROM publishing.

Another great cross-media company is Pearson, which includes in its portfolio newspapers, magazines and books, as well as both terrestrial and satellite television. Its newspapers include *The Financial Times* and the papers in the Westminster Press Group, while its book publishing interests encompass the 250-year old Longman empire, one of the great monuments of British publishing, and Penguin Books, among other less famous imprints.

Even from these brief accounts, it is clear that the competition between media is being conducted at least partly in the context of competition within companies. These global companies are a necessary response to global communications and information systems which are technologically independent of political boundaries. They do, however, raise important political questions about the regulatory regimes under which their different parts operate in different countries. Almost all of the book and newspaper publishing activities of these groups takes place under conditions which can loosely be described as being a 'free' press, but broadcasting and telecommunications regimes vary widely. One consequence is that, on the one hand, companies have to be aware of and conform to many different standards, and, on the other, they are able to do things in one market which would be illegal in another where they also operate. Some of the political and social implications of these issues will be pursued in Chapter 6.

THE MARKET: DEFINITION AND SIZE

The market in which publishing companies operate is one that is fairly well understood, although some other aspects of the information market have been less thoroughly described and analysed. In 1995, some 95,000 new titles or new editions were published in the UK, an increase, but by no means a startling increase, on the previous year. The total has increased by about one-third in a decade (in 1984 it was 51,500). Of the total output of British publishers in 1995, some 56,000 (both new titles and reprints) were paperbacks at an average price of £13.64. Overall, the largest category was fiction (9.1% of the whole), at an average price of £9.03 for hardbacks and £5.88 for paperbacks; hardback non-fiction had an average price of £18.88.

These figures are of some interest and importance, for they help us to define some of the most important characteristics of this sector of the information market-place. First, it deals with a very large number of what marketing experts call 'product lines'. The 95,000 editions are, of course, joining many of the 88,700 published in 1994, and some of the 82,300 published in 1993, as well as smaller numbers from earlier years, and books imported from abroad, especially the USA, where 139,300 editions were published in 1994. Since, in practice, few retail bookshops carry a stock of more than about 20,000 titles, there is much competition for a place on their shelves and hence for the attention of potential book-buyers. Of course, not all books are sold through book-shops, but some 70% of all sales by value in 1994 were to individual consumers, as against 30% to public and private sector institutions. As a market of some £1,990 million, the consumer book market is one worth fighting for.

Even these figures pale into comparative insignificance beside the circulation figures of newspapers and magazines. The mass circulation tabloids regularly attract daily sales of 5 million copies, and the most popular of the British broadsheets, *The Daily Telegraph*, sells over 1 million. In this context, the sales of books are small indeed. The magazine market is equally vibrant; in 1990, 31 titles from 7 publishers of women's magazines sold nearly 12 million copies. All of this, however, must be put into the context of the most popular mass medium of all. Television must attract millions of viewers to survive, especially in the case of the vast majority of channels that have no public subsidy or other non-commercial sources of revenue. In Britain, episodes of soap operas such as *Coronation Street* or *EastEnders* attract audiences of more than 10 million several times a week throughout the year.

Although television is a distinctive sector of the information market-place, it is related to the market for the printed word and for other information media. As we have seen in looking at how British newspapers have changed, there are multidirectional influences between different parts of the media. In broad terms, the reading of books has remained constant despite the vast popularity of television, but it is certainly not comparable with it. Surveys over the last 20 years have fairly consistently produced the same results; while 99% of the adult population watch television at some time during the week, fewer than 50% read a book. Moreover, while television viewing is consistent across socio-economic divides, book reading falls below 40% in social groups IV and V, rising to more than 65% in groups I and II. The consumer book market has a clear socio-economic bias towards the wealthier and better educated members of society, whereas television (in general terms, although not necessarily in terms of specific choices of viewing) transcends those boundaries.

Because of its size, the publishing sector links, and overlaps with, many other sectors of the information industry. At one end of the spectrum, it is in competition with newspapers, magazines and television; at the other, its competitors are CD-ROMs, online databases and the World Wide Web. Similarly, at the same time, it is part of the entertainment industry competing against other leisure pursuits from embroidery to mountain-climbing, and yet it is also part of the information industry competing with innovative software houses and state-of-the-art database hosts for the custom of currency dealers and transnational law firms.

As we have seen, the printed word has already been superseded in some parts of the information market-place. In 1992, nearly 4500 databases were available worldwide, through nearly 800 online hosts. About 200 organizations in the UK are either producing such databases or offering online services to customers. This, however, is trivial compared with the ever-increasing number of organizations, institutions and companies with their own sites on the World Wide Web. Of course, not all of this is purely commercial, but much of it is, even in public sector institutions. University libraries, for example, often charge 'customers' (even when, as is usually the case, these customers are members of the university) for making online searches, so that the boundaries between commercial and non-commercial, and public and private, would be becoming less clear with every year that passes, even if this were not also the general thrust of government policy in Britain and many other industrialized countries.

Moreover, the provision of electronic information is not entirely confined to the academic and commercial sectors. Most modern domestic televisions have a teletext facility, through which they can receive the broadcast digital signals of such services as ORACLE and CEEFAX. Usage of these services is not as high as their originators predicted, but they are nevertheless used.

Like television itself, they have the advantage of immediacy, and, unlike television, the viewer has some control over what is viewed. Scrolling through the database, or searching it using the index, is time-consuming and frustrating compared with using a CD-ROM with good software, but that is not the appropriate comparison. For the user who (typically) is looking for local or regional weather or travel information, public teletext services provide relatively easy access to information which is otherwise available only at some expense (perhaps by telephone), intermittently (when it is broadcast at the whim of the broadcasters), or not at all.

Recent developments suggest that teletext services will grow in importance in future years. Locally based services, some funded by advertising revenue, and others supported by local authorities or public-private sector joint ventures, are beginning to become more familiar. Unlike the national services, they tend to be in public places rather than in the home, providing, for example, information about local public transport services, environmental and planning information, or the sort of information and advice traditionally available from a Citizens' Advice Bureau, a tourist information centre or a public library. Terminals are sometimes accessible to the public, or sometimes used by intermediaries; in either case, they represent another electronic intrusion into the formerly protected world of print, and an electronic extension of access to information.

The convergence of information and communication technologies is leading to further developments which will fundamentally change some parts of the information market-place. Long after the USA, Britain is now being 'cabled' with wide-band optic fibre cables which can carry the full range of digital signals: audio (for telephone), visual (for television) and data (for multimedia services and interactive communications). There have been legal restrictions on the use of such networks; in particular, the principal telecommunications company in the UK was forbidden from entering the cable television market, but this will soon change. The creation of an information superhighway, a common-carrier network for digital signals, is already on the political agenda. Such a network is being developed in the USA, and western Europe will follow. In Britain, the networking of schools is a significant political issue, which seems likely to be resolved by involving one or more commercial network providers in a partnership between the public and private sectors. Domestically, and for most businesses, however, the key development is that of cable; although it is being installed to provide television services, the cable network is the basis of the British superhighway. Elsewhere, such as in Singapore, the infrastructure is already far advanced, with the intention of making a wide range of services available from homes and offices. The superhighway opens up a number of possibilities, some of which like home banking and home shopping are experimental only in the sense that the public use of them in real time is experimental; the technology is tried and tested. The revolution will be in communications, and in all those things which communications permit, inducing radical changes in the patterns of work and leisure even greater than those that have already happened.

FRAGMENTATION OR COMPETITION?

The fragmentation of the information market-place is, it seems, a necessary condition of this expansion and continuing growth. Within living memory, it consisted of little more than the printed word. It now contains a multitude of competing and complementary sectors. Although print continues to predominate in some of these, in others it is supplemented and in some it has been replaced. Others again are completely new; they are sectors into which the printed word never went and indeed could never go. Competition has introduced a sharper edge to the commercial element which has always been intrinsic in the process of information transfer. The new technologies all need massive investments, but they are developing so quickly that the investment is likely to be of comparatively short term value. The replacement of computer systems on a five-year cycle is well established throughout the industrialized world, but we are now also seeing the cyclical replacement of some parts of the infrastructure as well, with the development of new communications systems based on geostationary satellites and fibre optic cabling. The experience of the last 20 years suggests that the pace of change and of technological development will certainly not diminish and will probably increase.

The overtly competitive element has raised a whole range of issues which were formerly suppressed even when they were identified. Information has never been 'free', but now it can be realistically costed. To some extent this has always been possible; for example, the data which is now used to define the cost of each loan made by a public library has always been available, but methodologies for making use of it were only developed when the political and economic climate demanded that the information be obtained and used. Similar calculations can be made about almost any information transaction, with greater or lesser difficulty, and greater or lesser significance. Where realistic and meaningful costings of the transaction are possible, the temptation to pass them on to the end-user is often irresistible and may become mandatory. The new competitors in the information market-place do not share, or perhaps even understand, the benevolent desire to inform which is the common heritage of the traditional information providers, the librarians. Publishers have always known the cost of information, but even they disguised it to some extent, and only in the harsher climate of multinational corporations has publishing had to become the hard-edged business which it must now be to survive. Some of these issues and their implications are among the subjects of Chapters 4 and 5.

4

THE ECONOMIC DIMENSION
2 Access to information

It is comparatively easy to demonstrate that information is not free. A book borrowed from a public library may be 'free' to the user at the point at which the service is delivered, but the borrower is, in one way or another and with only rare exceptions, an indirect contributor to the cost of both the book and the library. It is not impossible to calculate the cost of each loan, and the information can even be put to meaningful use. Calculating cost, however, is only the starting-point. What is far more difficult is calculating *value*. In part, the problem is that such a calculation has to deal with a negative, the thorny problem of the loss which may be incurred by the absence of information. This can probably never be more than an approximation, but information providers who operate successfully in the more competitive parts of the market-place have long since realized that they can charge very high prices to those for whom the lack of information is a matter of concern. The user who needs instantaneous financial data will not query its cost until it manifestly exceeds the losses which would be incurred by not having access to it. It is on such a foundation that much of the information industry has been built.

The cultural change lies not so much in the solution of such problems (or perhaps more properly conundrums), but rather in the articulation of them. The development of new information technologies and information delivery systems has fundamentally changed the relationship between the supplier and consumer of information, and the role of the intermediary who comes between them. The traditional model distanced the consumer of information from the cost of providing it, even if it was the consumer who indirectly bore the cost. Moreover, there was an assumption, sometimes unexpressed, that the provision of information, especially in the form of books, was inherently desirable, and the role of the state or of other agencies was to facilitate rather than inhibit the information transfer process. Historically, this can be illustrated in two examples which are still of great contemporary importance.

THE PRICES OF BOOKS AND THE COST OF BROADCASTS

First, in many industrialized countries there has been, and in some there still is, a mechanism which partially regulates the prices of books. This can take many forms, but the most familiar model, which operated in the UK for most of the twentieth century, is that of setting a minimum price below which a book may not be sold. The Net Book Agreement, in which this was embodied in 1900 and in a slightly revised form in 1957, was designed to achieve two objectives: to sustain the profit margins of the retail booksellers and of the publishers, and to maintain a steady supply of books on a wide variety of subjects. As a matter of historical fact, it was the former consideration which lay behind the creation of the Agreement during the 1890s, but it was the latter which was the basis of the arguments which sought to justify it during the last 40 years of its existence.

The argument in favour of retail price maintenance on books, whether through the Net Book Agreement, or by similar mechanisms which operate in some other countries, is that books are a cultural as well as a commercial commodity, and that it is, therefore, culturally desirable that a wide variety of them should be available at reasonable prices and in many places. This it is argued, is inherently difficult because of the economics of book publishing, production and distribution, which were discussed briefly in Chapter 3. Profit margins in the book industry are indeed small, probably no more than about 10% for the publisher on an average title, and perhaps as little as 3% gross for each book sold by a retail bookseller. The case was that if there were price competition between booksellers these margins would prove to be inadequate. Bookshops would close, and the publishers be deprived of their only means of laying their wares before the public. Such shops as survived would only be able to sell highly profitable mass market books, and consequently publishers would no longer be willing to publish the wide range of books of cultural, scientific and educational value which they currently produce.

The surprising thing about this argument is not that it should have been put forward, but that it should have been accepted almost without question. When the Net Book Agreement apparently fell foul of British law in relation to restrictive trade practices, it was 'tried' in the Restrictive Practices Court in 1963, and allowed on cultural grounds along the lines suggested in the last paragraph. The argument for free market pricing was barely heard at all; when it was, it commanded no sympathy from the Court. Not until the mid-1990s did the Net Book Agreement come to an end, and then it was largely because a few major publishers and entrepreneurial booksellers effectively chose to ignore it. The consequences fell far short of the predicted cultural catastrophe, although there are early indications of significant changes in the retail book trade.

The broader significance of the Net Book Agreement, and of similar pricing mechanisms in other countries, is that, despite its purely commercial origins, it was consistently defended on the grounds of social utility and cultural desirability. This was not a marketing ploy by the publishers; it was widely and genuinely accepted at all levels of society that the book was a cultural device as well as being the subject of commercial transactions. Strangely, this argument was not applied to newspapers or to magazines, even when newspapers were closing under economic pressure and diversity of opinion in the press was being eroded. A not dissimilar argument, however, did underlie the organization of broadcasting in the UK from the 1920s to the 1950s, and to some extent still does. Although the BBC was never funded by taxation, the fee for the compulsory licence which provides the bulk of the Corporation's revenue is, in effect, a form of taxation. Listeners (and later viewers) did not pay for what they could afford, but a flat rate set at a level which almost everyone could afford. It is an anomaly which became even more marked after 1955 when programmes transmitted by the BBC's commercial competitors could only be legally received on apparatus which was licensed with money which funded the BBC. Like the defence of the Net Book Agreement, the broadcasting licence fee was ultimately justified on cultural grounds: it provided the basis for a diverse and high-quality public service. Whether or not these arguments (about either bookselling or broadcasting) were justified is, to a large extent, irrelevant. The fact is that they were generally accepted.

To some extent they still are, for the television licence (it is no longer required for the receipt of radio broadcasting only) still survives. Significantly, however, both were challenged in the 1980s more seriously than ever before in their history. The Net Book Agreement came under attack from within the book trade. It was inimical to the new and more aggressive style of marketing which many booksellers adopted, following the general trend of retailing during that decade. Waterstones, soon to be followed by other, more traditional booksellers like Dillons and W. H. Smiths, transformed the public image of the bookshop. Their shops were well-lit showcases for books, where customers were welcome to browse and a tolerably competent staff was available to help, to the gentle strains of Vivaldi (also on sale in the CD section) in the background. Terry Maher, one of the pioneers of this new style of bookselling in the Pentos Group (which included

Dillons) tried by all means at his disposal to undermine the Net Book Agreement. He initially failed, despite a reference to the Monopolies Commission, an investigation by the Consumers' Association, and unfavourable noises from the European Union about its legislation against anti-competitive practices. Only in 1993 did a government minister take up the theme, and begin to make the apparently obvious link between the abrogation of the Net Book Agreement and the free market economic theories which had dominated British political thought and policy since 1979. The end came in 1993, but by implosion rather than assault.

The recent history of the television licence is more political, but no less odd or instructive. The BBC has always proudly maintained a tradition of independence from government, although this has perhaps sometimes worn a little thin when under serious strain at times of national emergency. Broadly speaking, however, there is more reality than pretence in this stance, and certainly the Corporation's journalists and reporters have a highly developed talent for annoying politicians just as their colleagues in the printed media do. Unlike print journalists, however, BBC journalists are working for an organization the bulk of whose revenue still comes from a form of payment whose level is determined by the government. It is this that puts the BBC in the political firing line.

During the late 1980s and early 1990s, the television industry has undergone fundamental change. The franchises to operate the independent terrestrial stations in Britain were redistributed (as they are periodically) on entirely commercial grounds. At the same time, the granting of the first licences for satellite television introduced a new and powerful competitor. The position of an autonomous public service broadcaster, supported by a compulsory levy on the owners of television sets regardless of whether or not they used its services, became even more anomalous.

The political arguments about the funding of the BBC (which

no doubt have many years to run) and those about the Net Book Agreement (which are now essentially complete) have some important similarities. Both take place in an arena whose boundaries are being redefined by the diversification and fragmentation of the information market-place. The cultural argument no longer commands universal assent among politicians or voters, or even within the two industries themselves. The partial control of book prices, and the non-commercial basis of the funding of a substantial part of the broadcasting industry, are both survivals which seem increasingly out of place. The intense competition to supply information and entertainment to consumers is taking place in a commercial ethos in which cultural considerations seem to count for little.

THE COST OF LIBRARIES

The second example of the historic model of the state's generally benevolent attitude towards the information market-place is to be found in public libraries. The public library has become one of the symbols, even perhaps one of the icons, of a 'civilized' society. It is provided, like basic education and social welfare, by using the product of general taxation to fund particular services. The public library pioneers of the nineteenth century, whether they were philanthropists, well-wishers, political supporters or even librarians, saw public libraries as being for the public good, promoting literacy, education and culture. They became an integral part of the cultural fabric, and were soon to be found in virtually every town and in many villages. Although it was not until 1964 that local authorities in England and Wales were *obliged* to provide a public library service of an acceptable standard, in practice almost all had done so for decades.

What was less often appreciated, and rarely discussed, was that the public libraries were also an integral part of the economic fabric of the book trade. Even now, after many years of restraint and cutbacks, public libraries in the UK are spending over £100 million a year on books, the equivalent of nearly £2.00 per capita for the population of the UK as a whole. Although this is less than 5% of the total UK book market, it is not insignificant, and in some sectors (such as hardback fiction) the public libraries are actually the core market for the publishers. The involvement of the public libraries in the commercial world of publishing, even if only as customers, always had implications for their role. So too did their tradition of providing services free at the point of delivery. Even in the 1964 Public Libraries Act, this tradition was marginally challenged. Libraries were allowed to charge for certain services to which a cost could be attached, such as borrowing books from other libraries on behalf of users, or providing photocopies. Even more significantly, many libraries began to charge for non-printed media, such as recorded music and, in later years, videos and computer software. Once again, there was an unspoken assumption about the significance, and perhaps even the superiority, of the book. It is unnecessary, for these purposes, to argue whether or not that assumption might have been (or indeed might still be) justified. It is, however, important to notice it, for it was the advent of new media, challenging the book as a tool of entertainment and education, which forced librarians to rethink their attitude to charging their users.

The great majority of librarians, and apparently of politicians, still oppose charging for the 'core services' provided by public libraries, and will, no doubt, continue (at least in the case of the librarians) to do so. It is a theme to which we shall return towards the end of this Chapter. For the present we need only note that the reopened debate about the funding of the public library service has been impelled, in part, by the implications of the new media of information and communication.

PUBLIC GOOD OR PRIVATE PROFIT?

These examples are intended to illustrate two points which they have in common. First, they show the changing relationship between information providers and information consumers. Both sides are aware that their relationship now exists in an overtly commercial context, and in a general economic and political climate in which that context is emphasized. Common-user services, like broadcast television or public libraries, no longer have a monopoly, and can no longer be assumed to be the only paradigms of information delivery or domestic entertainment, any more than the book trade and the publishing industry can continue to assume that they have a uniquely important product. The assignment of costs and value to information itself, as well as to the systems for delivering it, has fundamentally changed our perception of both the product and the service

Secondly, a consideration of both book pricing and public library provision illustrates the historically benevolent role of the state in the information transfer process. By permitting a price control regime which was designed to protect certain kinds of culturally or educationally desirable publishing, or supporting a broadcasting organization which had a commitment to high-quality public service programming, the state gave a *de facto* endorsement to those products and services. The provision of services which are free at the point of delivery and which actually compete with charged services (as 'free' public libraries could be argued to compete with booksellers), is an equally remarkable example. It is probable that such benevolent regimes would have changed in any case, but during the 1980s a combination of political, economic and technological factors made the need to consider change even more urgent.

The political factors varied in their details in different countries, but the overall thrust was similar across the industrialized world. In summary, there was a move away from a centralist model, with a significant public sector which was essentially driven by needs, towards a more diffused model, with a heavy emphasis on the development of an entrepreneurial private sector which was market-driven. Nowhere was this change more marked than in the UK, where almost 40 years of consensus government (despite shifts between the left and the right) had created a widespread sense of corporatism in the state. The policies which prevailed from 1979 to 1997 led to the return of large parts of the public sector into private hands; for our purposes the most important of these was the telecommunications system, which was privatized in 1984. At the same time, a commitment to competition opened up the market. Again, this was true of telecommunications, where the privatized British Telecom was subject to competition which had not disturbed its nationalized predecessor, just as the BBC and the franchisees of commercial television were subjected to the less controlled competition of the satellite broadcasters. Market-oriented ideologies also formed the theoretical basis of the objections to the Net Book Agreement, and provided its opponents with some degree of political support.

ELECTRONIC COMMUNICATIONS: ACCESS AND COSTS

Political and economic factors thus converged, but even closer was the link between economics and technology. It was during the 1980s that some of the long-heralded benefits of the information technology revolution at last began to be felt, as ideas were translated into reality. The computer became a familiar object in the office and the library, and in many homes. It was widely used for a great variety of educational, professional and entertainment purposes, quite apart from the 'hidden' use of computer technology in retailing, manufacturing, transport and many other sectors of the economy. The wider use of computers, however, transformed the nature of the economic relationship between information providers and information consumers. The very nature of computer systems, especially when they were used to draw information from distant databases, meant that a cost could be assigned to each individual information transaction. In a library, it is only possible to give an average, and therefore notional, costing of a traditional transaction such as a loan; when information is sought from an online database, however, it is possible to give a precise costing of both the information itself (if it is charged for) and the telecommunications costs. There are still fixed costs for equipment and staff, which have to be added and are as vague as the notional costing of traditional services but the direct financial transactions which take place do allow a very specific cost to be quantified for one part of the operation. It is but a short step from here to the concept of a 'value-added' service, in which the information intermediary passes on to the consumer the costs incurred in obtaining the information from the supplier. What was once a purely service relationship has become a relationship between buyer and seller.

It is not only, however, in obviously value-added transactions that technology has changed the relationship between the provider and the recipient of information. The information chain itself has been radically changed, and new participants have taken the place of traditional players. In particular, the intermediary roles are different. In the familiar chain of communication from author to reader, only the roles of these two, at either end of the chain, remain substantially unmodified, and even their perceptions of each other and of their relationship have begun to change. In the traditional model, as we have seen, the author completes the work, and hands it over to those who will take technical, financial and commercial responsibility for its production, distribution and sale. The ultimate beneficiaries, the readers, are passive recipients at the end of this process, able to obtain only what those who stand between them and the author want them to have. Technology has wrought a fundamental change in this model.

A simple paradigm of a newer model can be found in the increasingly familiar systems of electronic mail ('e-mail'), and the discussion groups ('listservers') which are associated with these systems. An e-mail system, as its name suggests, is a computer-based substitute for traditional paper-based postal services. Subscribers have an e-mail address, which a central computer can use to route incoming messages to the recipient. The subscriber's messages are stored in a file in the computer; when the recipient logs on, they can be accessed by means of 'passwords', unique numbers similar to the PINs (Personal Identification Numbers) used for cashcards in automatic bank tellers. The recipient can then reply to the message, store it, print it, send it on to others, and sometimes choose other options. In this sense, e-mail is indeed merely a postal service, but the processing capacity of the computers which run the system allow it to become far more than that.

It is also possible to establish a group address (known as a 'nick-name' or 'alias'), so that a single message will automatically be sent to all members of a predetermined group. This is now common in many organizations as a substitute for the traditional internal memorandum which was once so familiar. Anyone in the group can use the system to contact every other member of the group, but each of them can also communicate privately both with the originator of the group message and with each other. It is only a short step from group addresses to the semi-public discussion groups which are now common in the academic world, and which are beginning to trespass on the territory previously occupied only by more formal systems of information transfer.

Discussion groups are set up by one or more individuals using an e-mail system, and subscriptions are then invited from anyone else who is interested in joining them, forming the electronic equivalent of a mailing list. At first, the process of assembling was done by word of mouth, but so many such groups now exist that it is becoming common to circulate members of existing lists in order to attract subscribers to a new list which might interest some of the same people. There is scope in this for commercial competition but we shall see that, in practice, this is not yet a factor. Messages are sent from members of the group to the e-mail address of the listserver, and then automatically re-routed to all subscribers. They are then stored with the subscriber's other e-mail messages to be read when the user next logs on to the system.

Listservers are being used in several ways. First, they are a very efficient means of disseminating information rapidly among a group of people with common interests. Some, for example, are now being used to advertise job vacancies, calls for research proposals and similar time-limited activities, in the academic world. In other words, the listserver can substitute for, or supplement, traditional print-on paper systems of information. Secondly, the listservers can be used to gather information. A subscriber can ask for help or advice, such as a bibliographic reference, an elusive fact, or the address or telephone number of someone known to the inquirer only by name. This function goes significantly beyond any conventional paper-based system; it is interactive, in the sense that the listserver exploits the communications network by allowing recipients to reply. This can be done either as a group message, through the listserver itself, or directly to the enquirer through an ordinary e-mail message.

The third use, which is more sophisticated, is to employ the listserver for the discussion of some issue of common interest. A subscriber poses a question to other members of the group, or proposes a theory or expounds an idea. Other members of the group can react and respond, while some may choose to be passive observers of a particular interchange. This is quite different from the simple model of a mailing system, or even an interactive information and enquiry service. Used in this way, the listserver creates a computer-based forum for semi-public discourse. Perhaps the nearest traditional analogy is that of the correspondence columns of a newspaper, but the comparison is not a close one. The manager of the listserver does not exercise editorial control; the redistribution of each message is automatic, and is in exactly the form in which it is keyboarded and sent by the contributor. No-one has the authority to stop or interfere with a particular interchange, and everyone has the right to intervene in it. If the letters page of *The Times* fails to provide an adequate model for the functions of the listserver, perhaps we should consider another possibility: the questions and discussion which follow a public speech. There are some parallels, but they are very limited. Discussion is controlled (by a chairperson, and probably by some sort of agreed rules of procedure), and the time available for it is limited. It is not normally recorded in any permanent form, and can only rarely be resumed at a later time.

NETWORKS: AN ELECTRONIC DEMOCRACY?

The difficulty of finding a traditional communication system with which the listservers can be compared is in itself a measure of the innovation which they represent. In effect, an electronic discussion group, using a listserver, is a wholly new kind of communication system. It combines some aspects of printed communication, such as letters to the press and perhaps newsletters, with the use of the telephone and private correspondence, with e-mail, and with oral presentations and discussions. To these, it has added its own unique features. These include the ability of the recipient to participate in the discussion at will, without control, and without having to attract the attention of any intermediary with an editorial or controlling role. Such discussions can take place without limitations of time or place, and can be started by any subscriber. This is, it would seem, electronic democracy at work.

The basic principle of the electronic discussion group is extensible to the limit of the information technology which support it, and that is, indeed, the great limitation. The systems which have been briefly described in the last few paragraphs are now familiar to many academic and professional groups, and are to be found also in government and in large institutions and organizations. For many users they are 'free'. In Britain, the USA and other western countries, governments, research organizations and the universities (or their funding agencies) support the computing and communications networks which facilitate the operation of the system without direct charge to end-users. These networks are complex and expensive. They are dependent on a sophisticated infrastructure which includes mainframe computers with massive processing and storage capacity, usually at each major site of usage (each university, for example), as well as effective telecommunications systems (sometimes along specially dedicated lines) to link them. Each mainframe is linked locally to workstations from which individual users access the system. The infrastructure itself has to be installed, maintained and regularly enhanced as usage increases and the technology is constantly changed and improved.

The origin of the networks was almost casual, but it has now been formalized. In Britain, JANET links the universities and other academic bodies, and, in a more advanced form, as SuperJANET, is widely available to subscribers and can carry far more data and multimedia formats. International links between national and regional systems have created the Internet, originally sponsored by the National Science Foundation in the USA, which now links millions of users through hundreds of thousands of computers across the world. The Internet has revolutionized communications in the academic world, and has the potential to change them yet further as we shall see. But its existence and operation raise a whole range of questions which will have to be answered. Not the least of these are those of cost and of funding, for there is no reason to suppose that the Internet and its constituent parts, any more than public libraries, will continue to be regarded as a service which should, as a social good, be provided 'free'.

Not surprisingly, the private sector proved to be initially somewhat less enthusiastic about e-mail and its associated facilities than have academics and others in primarily public sector environments. There are commercial systems which give access to the Internet. There are also public e-mail systems to which individuals and companies can subscribe, in much the same way as they can subscribe for telephone services; indeed, one of the major systems in the UK (BT Internet) is run by British Telecom which still dominates the general domestic and commercial telecommunications market. These systems are now widely used, for there are clear commercial advantages. In particular, e-mail permits easy communications between time zones. To make a telephone call from London to Los Angeles during ordinary business hours in both cities is almost impossible; at 5.00 p.m. in London, it is 9.00 a.m. in Los Angeles. When there are also the complications of different working weeks (in Islamic countries, for example, where the weekend is normally Thursday and Friday or Friday and Saturday), the problem is even more acute. E-mail overcomes this; the message is sent during normal hours, and is read when the recipient next accesses the system. The reply can then be generated and sent; it will be waiting when the original sender next logs on. Thus, for example, a message can be sent from London at noon on Monday, and can be read in Sydney at 9.00 a.m. on Tuesday (eleven hours later); an immediate reply can be read in London at 9.00 a.m. on Wednesday. In the interchange, no-one has had to make or take telephone calls at hours of the night when they might not be functioning at their best; on the other hand, airmail would be slower (by several days) and fax would be less secure, since an e-mail message can only go directly from sender to recipient because of the password protection of the file stores in each person's computer. Such advantages have commended themselves to many businesses, and the use of e-mail and its associated facilities can be expected to continue to grow.

Similarly, the listservers and electronic groups are beginning to supplant some other traditional means of communications. At a time when the costs of travel and accommodation are, in real terms, increasing more quickly than the costs of communications, electronic substitutes for meetings and conferences are inevitably attractive. Some academic conferences make use of these facilities, so that, for example, those who are unable to attend the conference for some reason can read a pre-circulated paper on a discussion list, and join in the discussion by the same means or by registering for a specially established group name for a particular conference. This may not be as satisfactory, in some ways, as being present at a meeting, but it is better than not being able to participate at all. Similar uses in the public service and in business are increasingly common.

THE WORLD WIDE WEB: THE FUTURE?

Electronic mail, listservers and associated activities such as electronic conferencing are all comparatively informal communications networks, in the sense that there is no real editorial control over input, and they can be – and in the academic world often are – made accessible to anyone who wishes to participate. In that sense, they have added a new dimension to the dissemination and communication of information.

Perhaps the most dramatic change of all, however, is that inherent in the development of the World Wide Web (WWW). The Web, like the Internet itself, has its origin in the scientific research community, in this case at CERN, the European nuclear research facility in Geneva, Switzerland. The Web is based on the ability of hypermedia systems to provide direct links between one file or one part of a file and another. The creator of a file on the Web (a 'Website') builds in 'hot links' to other pages which, by a click on the mouse, allows the user to move to that page. This may be a page on the same site or it may be elsewhere; the possibilities are limitless, and indeed the location of the information is of no concern to the end-user. Sites themselves have Internet addresses, derived from the system used for e-mail addresses. Websites are identified by Uniform Resource Locators (URLs), which provide a global access system, analogous to (but far less organized than) internationally recognized telephone numbers.

It is now normal practice for almost all large organizations and many smaller ones to have their own Websites. They have become an integral part of the information and marketing strategy of everything from airlines to zoos. Simultaneously, a whole new Web-based culture has developed. Individuals can establish their own sites (or 'home pages') and use them to provide whatever information or opinion they choose. All that is needed is access to a host computer ('server') linked to the Internet, and the very basic technical skills needed to use hypertext mark-up language (HTML), the programming code in which most Web data is written. Browsing this new and fascinating global data bank has become, for some people, a hobby that verges on an obsession, and – significantly – has attracted the metaphor of the classic Californian activity of surfing.

The World Wide Web, however, is more than merely an advertising tool or a toy. It has vast implications for the future of information service provision and the communication of information. In effect, the 'owner' of the site (or 'Webmaster') is a publisher, but a publisher upon whom there are no significant external controls.[1] The quality control – even at the level of basic factual accuracy – that traditionally typifies all but the most ephemeral and peripheral publishing, is completely lacking from the Web. All that exists is a voluntary constraint imposed by Webmasters on

---

[1] Of course, the usual laws of libel, obscenity and intellectual property apply (for which see Chapter 6), but they are even less than usually enforceable in the case of Websites, as we shall see.

themselves, or by site owners on their Webmasters. Individuals can – and do – publish whatever they want. Whether this is electronic democracy at work, or merely a worthless electronic anarchy, it has certainly become in part the electronic equivalent of vanity publishing, but without incurring any significant direct costs and with an automatic global distribution system.

The exponential growth of the Web and indeed of the Internet as a whole has created its own problems. The superhighway is all too often like an overcrowded and undersized city street in the rush hour, with traffic barely moving and offering little more than frustration and mounting costs for travellers. For all its universality, the Internet is fragile and vulnerable. The demand for network usage is growing more quickly than the physical infrastructure which sustains it, and response times from URLs are often unacceptably slow, especially outside the comparatively protected sphere of the academic networks. Moreover, the system, like a grid system which supplies electric power, can be exposed to domino-like failures. In the summer of 1997, two interlinked computer crashes in Virginia brought a large part of the Internet to a halt for nearly 24 hours, with repercussions across the globe. The reliability of both the information itself and the information system cannot be guaranteed, and the inevitably continuing reliance on the Internet will further expose its potential weaknesses.

It is, however, possible to use networks more formally and in more limited applications, by controlling input and by limiting the capacity of recipients to respond. The system which best explains this model of usage is that of the *electronic journal*, a form of communication which has existed experimentally for over a decade, but which is now beginning to come into its own in some fields.

ELECTRONIC PUBLISHING: TOWARDS A NEW PARADIGM?

The basic principle of the electronic journal is derived from the traditional model of the scholarly or scientific periodical. Such periodicals all operate in a basically similar way, although there are differences between disciplines. Contributors submit papers for publication, usually based on recent research or perhaps on a review of previous work in the field; the editor reads the submissions, or (more often) sends each to one or more specialist advisers ('referees') who will assess its suitability for publication. The paper may then be rejected, accepted as it stands, or (very commonly) returned to the contributor for revisions in the light of the referees' comments. In due course, it is accepted in its final version, and printed in the next available issue of the journal. The whole process may take between three and twelve months depending on the subject matter, the importance of the paper and the traditions of different academic disciplines, as well as less predictable factors such as the efficiency of the editor and the willingness of potential referees to undertake the work. This is the classic model of scholarly communication; it has served the academic world well for over a century.

The earliest experiments with electronic journals (or *online* journals as they were often, and significantly, called) tried to convert this model into an electronic format. Contributors submitted their papers electronically to a computer which could be accessed by the editor. The editor read the paper in this form, and perhaps sent it to a referee's computer; the referee's comments were returned electronically to the editor, who transmitted them, perhaps suitably modified and certainly anonymized (as is the custom with referees' reports) to the authors. In other words, the traditional process was simply replicated in electronic form, including an electronic version of the quality control which is the reason for the editing and refereeing process.

All of this was comparatively easy, and has become easier with the growth of the public access networks. Contributors, editors and referees can communicate using the Internet, to which, almost without exception, they will have unlimited access. Most potential readers are in the same position. It is, however, precisely at this final and crucial stage, when the work is to be transmitted to the reader, that the real difficulties begin. This is another electronic equivalent of publication, but once again no simple substitution of electronic for paper-based methods is possible. To understand the problem it is necessary to consider how scholarly and scientific journals are traditionally published and distributed.

Traditional learned journals are owned by publishers, who are either publishing houses or learned societies, or sometimes the two working together. Editors and referees (and occasionally contributors) may receive small fees for their work, although this is not a major factor either for the publishers or for the editors and referees: the fees are small, because the real rewards lie in the academic recognition (which may generate financial rewards in other ways, such as by promotion) rather than money. The real costs to the publisher lie in printing and distribution. Typically, the journal is published between four and six times a year, and the annual issues are cumulated into a volume, usually with an index. Print runs are often small (as low as 250 in some cases), but distribution is worldwide. On the other hand, money for subscriptions (almost all of it from libraries) is collected annually in advance to provide working capital; distribution is undertaken by agents who make their own profits by charging a premium for the services which they provide. The economics of journal publishing are by no means impossible, but journals have nevertheless, and with some justification, become very expensive, with subscriptions of several hundred pounds being by no means uncommon. As a result, in times of economic constraint, many libraries have been forced to cancel subscriptions, thus further decreasing the print runs and increasing the prices.

Conceptually, it is not difficult to design a system which could replace printed publication by electronic distribution, and even to devise mechanisms of charging and payment to support the operation. In practice, however, there is a major obstacle. The scholarly communication system which has developed around the refereed journal has come to occupy a place of central importance in the academic world. Individual academics, and their departments and universities, are judged for many purposes by the quality and even the quantity of their published output. When that output is in the pages of a journal which is known to be strictly controlled to the highest standards by editors and referees, it is particularly prestigious and can have a major influence on individual and institutional success.

The system depends largely on peer-group acceptance of it, although there are some allegedly more objective measures which can be used. The most important of these are derived from citation indexes which show the number of citations of a particular paper in other publications. In practice, however, it is publication in the 'right' journals which really matters, and several investigations in recent years have suggested that scientists and others are reluctant to accept electronic journals as being the equivalent, in qualitative terms, of traditional print-on-paper learned journals. This is partly because there is some suspicion of the strictness of the refereeing, partly because of concerns about the permanence of the journal itself, and partly because of the fear that electronically published papers will not be so widely accessible, and hence not be so widely cited, as papers published in the traditional format. As a result, there is evidence that electronic journals do not attract high-quality papers, that therefore they have not themselves become prestigious, and that, consequently, they continue to fail to attract the very papers which alone could improve their prestige. This vicious circle has been partly caused by the general reluctance to change, which is no less common among the most innovative of intellectuals than it is elsewhere in society, but some causes are more rational, and are essentially related to the distribution and access mechanisms of the electronic journal.

The essence of the distribution system of the traditional journal is that it is bought by libraries on subscription, and is thus available to all the users of a particular library. Moreover, individual papers are accessible to the users of non-subscribing libraries through interlibrary lending or document delivery systems, which usually involve the provision, for private use, of a photocopy of a particular paper. The economics of journal publication leaves few margins for error, but the system does work, and it is possible to publish scientific and learned journals at a price which the market will tolerate. The calculations do not, however, easily accommodate radical change, especially of the size and scale implicit in switching from paper-based to electronic publication and dissemination.

A traditional journal is paid for in much the same way as a book; it is true that the payment is a subscription, but the basic principle – buying an information carrier which becomes a common-user tool – is the same. Only in a very limited way can anything like this apply to an electronic journal. One model for such a journal is that 'subscribers' buy access to the database in which the papers are held, and, as in accessing any other database, pay for both the telecommunications charge and for access to the information itself. Such charges might be paid by an individual or by an institution, but even in this simple model there has already been a critical shift of emphasis. The traditional journal is bought by a library for general access; individual usages of it are neither quantified nor costed in normal circumstances, as we have already seen in the slightly different, but fundamentally similar, case of public library usage. Access to an electronic journal, however, can be very precisely costed, and identified with a particular library user. Who shall pay the charges which are incurred? Whatever the answer (which is determined by a combination of political and economic factors) we no longer have here a model of common access to a common resource.

This is partly because the economic model on which an electronic journal is based is quite different from that of a traditional printed journal. There are, of course, some parallels. The database, in this model, is owned by a publisher, just as a publisher owns the title and often the copyright in the papers of the traditional journal. The publisher of the database, like the traditional journal publisher, takes financial risks in order to produce the journal. These risks are high, but the income is no longer either so predictable or so conveniently collected. Under the traditional system, the annual advance subscription means that the print run need not exceed the demand. Indeed, it is normally tailored to it almost exactly, so that there are few spare copies, and individual. issues of the journal go 'out of print' almost as soon as they are published. The money to support this operation is received in advance of costs being incurred; typically, subscriptions fall due on 1 January, and a quarterly is normally published in March, June, September and December. Printing and distribution costs for the year are not even incurred until the bulk of the subscription income has been received, and some of it can be held back (earning interest) for as long as 12 months.

No such certainty is possible for the publisher of an electronic journal offering instantaneous access to a continuously augmented database. First, the publisher must buy (or rent) sufficient computer storage space not merely for the current issue, but for all previous issues of the journal. This is essential if the electronic journal is to compete with the prestige of the printed journal which, despite going out of print almost immediately after it is published, is nevertheless available in libraries or through document delivery services in perpetuity. With an electronic journal, this permanent availability can be achieved only by permanent electronic storage. It is possible to devise models in which this would be possible without occupying large amounts of expensive space in potentially interactive file stores. CD-ROM is one obvious mechanism for a halfway house between electronic and printed storage for longer-term access, and is increasingly used. Even so, the advocates and producers of electronic journals are still confronted by a real problem: the use of an essentially ephemeral communications technology for the permanent storage of data which may be intermittently and unpredictably required over long periods of time.

On the other hand, the 'online' model is not the only way in which an electronic journal system can be envisaged. Another experimental model has a central file store from which the papers for many different journals can be retrieved, offering an electronic surrogate for a document delivery system rather than for a single journal. Again, there are inevitable economic issues to be resolved, but moving closer to the model of a library rather than a publisher at least opens up the possibility of public sector involvement. In Britain, such a model is under serious consideration, partly in response to the ever-tightening limits on library budgets at a time when the quantity of research is increasing and the output of academic literature continues to burgeon. At present, the electronic journal may be thought of as an interesting example of a technology that works, but whose application is being delayed by commercial and human factors. The delay, however, seems likely to be a temporary one as financial necessity overwhelms both the publishers and the purchasers of the traditional printed product. The long-term solution seems likely to be that access will be controlled by password, and that the password itself, and perhaps each usage of it, will be subject to charges by the information provider, or 'publisher'.

There is already what might be regarded as a modified form of the electronic journal, which has some of its characteristics as well as some of those of electronic conferencing and e-mail, which has been a considerable success. This is the so-called *bulletin board*. As its name suggests, this is a good deal less formal than a journal, but at the same time it is slightly more so than a discussion group. Information on a particular subject is sent to an editor, by e-mail (or indeed by any other means), and is stored by the editor in the bulletin board's central file store, usually held in a mainframe computer. The information is edited, as in a traditional newsletter, with which a bulletin board is, in some ways, comparable. The bulletin board itself may be subdivided into sections, have a contents 'page', or an index, have facilities for searching and so on. Access is through a network, exactly like e-mail, and may be either free or charged. Typically, would-be users gain network access through the mainframe to which their own workstations are connected, and then 'call' a number or code which links the workstation to the file containing the bulletin board.

For users with network access, the system is both cheap and simple; its advantages are many. An electronic bulletin board, unlike the traditional newsletter with which it might be compared, can be updated continuously. Access is efficient, because the user can ignore all those parts which are of no interest. Material can often be downloaded for local storage for future reference or for printing to be conventionally filed. Some bulletin board editors use the listservers to inform their user communities of updates, alterations and other developments. Especially in the academic world, with almost universal uncharged access to network facilities, bulletin boards have proved to be very successful. Many now take the form of regularly updated Websites, or have interfaces which simulate the increasingly familiar appearance of a Web page.

Electronic mail, electronic discussion groups, the World Wide Web and electronic journals and bulletin boards have been explored at some length because they illustrate both the potential and the limitations of the use of information technology. All of them offer great advantages over the traditional methods of information storage and transfer which they have replaced, or indeed offer facilities which no traditional system could have provided. The most important difference is probably that of immediacy. Electronic communications are, for all practical purposes, instantaneous; the delays caused by 'traffic jams' in the network, or temporary overload on individual computers, are comparatively trivial compared with the delay in publishing traditional newsletters, printed journals and books.

Moreover, all of these systems, to a greater or lesser extent, allow some form of participation in an active relationship rather than mere passive reception of information. At one end of the scale, e-mail and discussion lists are, by definition, interactive, but anyone can contribute material for editing into a bulletin board, and the electronic journal is as accessible as its printed equivalents within appropriate communities. The Internet makes all public information in the system widely available. By exploiting various devices ('search engines') which permit unlimited and uncharged access and searching on a worldwide basis, it is possible to find bulletin boards, discussion lists, and the 'archived' products of public electronic discourse by using any computer with network access.

The development of the international academic network (which took less than five years) is perhaps the greatest revolution in scholarly communications since the fifteenth century, but no revolution is without its disadvantages. There are some less favourable factors to be considered. The use of all the systems which have been described depends on access to a network which links the individual user to the computer in which the information which is being sought is stored, or which facilitates the communication which is being attempted. At one level this is familiar. We expect to need, and to subscribe for, a telephone before being able to make telephone calls. We expect to pay the cost of postage when sending a letter. Indeed, we expect to pay an appropriate price when we buy a book or subscribe to a journal or newsletter, but we have also developed systems which allow books and journals to be bought at general expense using public funds, in return for general access in libraries. It is this transaction, and the social and cultural assumptions and expectations which underpin it, which is being challenged by the electronic systems we have discussed in this chapter.

The true cost of network access is high; this is not altered by the fact that, for the majority of users, it is hidden. Moreover, some technical skills are needed in order to gain access, although they are basic and simple. More importantly, however, the potential user needs some understanding of the operation of the network and of the structure of the information itself in order to use it effectively. Although the knowledge base and skill level are of no higher order than those needed to use a book, they are not instinctive even in users of high intelligence who are familiar with other information media. Just as we have to be taught to read and write, and how to use a table of contents or an index, we have to be taught how to search a database, use an e-mail system or participate in an electronic discussion group. These are indeed skills which, once acquired, seem so basic as barely to be skills at all, but, like all skills, they have the effect of excluding those who do not possess them. Network access and skill development can both present some obstacle to the use of electronic information and communications systems.

THE COST OF ACCESS: ISSUES AND PROBLEMS

The most important obstacle, however, remains the cost. As has been suggested throughout this chapter, there is a fundamental difference between buying a book and buying information from a database. The latter is acquired once and can be used once only, the former, once acquired, can be used – for all practical purposes – for ever by anyone. We can ascribe the cost of a particular information transaction to the person by whom, or for whom, the transaction was undertaken. Information is no longer even perceived to be 'free' in an economic sense, however 'free' access may be in the sense that there is no legal or technical obstacle to obtaining it. The partial concealment of the cost of electronic information access through a publicly funded network does not affect the central issue, and may, in any case, be assumed to be a temporary phenomenon. We are again led towards the concept of the value which is added to information by the transactions which carry it from source to user. This value can also be costed and the end-user can therefore be charged for the transaction as a whole.

The possibility of making profits from the provision of information to individuals, by charging for information itself and for the means of obtaining it, has made great changes in the way in which we think about such provision. The traditional liberal assumptions, suggested in the first part of this chapter, are no longer as applicable as once they were. The boundaries between private and public territories, and between personal and institutional domains, have shifted dramatically. In political terms, this has expressed itself in the move from the public to the private sector which has already been mentioned, but this is merely one manifestation of a change which is driven as much by technology as it is by public policy. As the private sector takes a larger role in information provision, and as it becomes easier to assess the cost of providing information services, questions can be formulated about the role of the public sector with its apparently 'free' provision of some of the same services. In British political discourse, this question is usually addressed in terms of the definition of the public library service. Although this is, in one sense, a special case, it does also have broader and more generally applicable implications. Public libraries operate under legislation which requires them to offer an adequate service, without defining what that service is. More recent legislation, made by Order-in-Council in 1991, specifically allows them to charge for certain services, including loan services of recorded music and videos, and interlibrary loans, as well as for value-added service such as online searching. The 1991 Order is permissive rather than mandatory, and there are variations between library authorities in their use of it, but charges for such services are now common.

In itself, this raises some general issues. Video hire, for example, is a lucrative business; it has been developed in the private sector, generally by small local shops. Public libraries which appear to compete in this market could be argued to have an unfair advantage from their publicly funded infrastructure and economies of scale. In practice, the range of videos available is probably different in the two outlets, and indeed a typical video hire shop probably has a significantly larger number of videos available than almost any library. The point of principle, however, remains. In some ways, the issue is similar to that raised by the competition between the BBC funded by a general levy on the viewing public, and the independent terrestrial and satellite channels funded from advertising and sponsorship. The question is no longer whether the public and private sectors should compete against each other, but rather whether there should be a public, or quasi-public, sector at all.

In the British public library arena, this issue increasingly revolves around the definition of the so-called 'core' services, which all political parties are committed to continuing to provide free at the point of delivery. If it is to be little more than a basic lending and reference service from the stock in any given library, this represents a significant reduction in the level of non-charged services available to many users, such as those who use small branches or mobile libraries. If all but the most basic services are moved out of the dimension of public provision, the implication is that the private sector will provide whatever the market will sustain, but only to those who can afford to buy information services at whatever price the market will bear.

Public libraries have responded to this changing environment in different ways. Some are unashamedly competing, especially in the provision of information to business industry and local government, and are working with the private sector and with other public sector agencies (such as university libraries, for example) in partnerships which provide high-quality services to those who seek and can afford high-value information. In other sectors, information service provision has slipped away from the public libraries, and much information which central and local government is statutorily obliged to provide is channelled through other agencies such as the Department of Social Security, or the environmental and planning departments of local authorities. The public libraries are thus losing their claim to a monopoly of public information provision, even at local level. In such circumstances, it is inevitable that those who cannot afford access to information through the services provided in the private sector will, eventually, have difficulty in obtaining certain kinds of information at all. This mismatch between needs, wants and provision will be investigated in Chapter 5.

The potential for conflict (as well as competition) between the public and private sectors in library and information service delivery is not, however, confined to the public library arena. The developments which we have discussed in the communications systems which link groups of scholars, both formal (such as electronic journals) and informal (such as e-mail), call into question the role of the library in the academic community. Traditionally hailed as the heart of the university, at least in academic rhetoric, the library is in danger of becoming little more than a textbook centre, bookstore and studying space. As information technology takes more information direct to academics' and students' desks through the computers which sit on them, the library becomes just another part of the network through which they meet their information needs.

All of these matters eventually coalesce into a single issue: access to information. Technology has improved the potential for access, but at the same time it has also provided the means for restricting it. The restrictions can be determined by technical skills, technological infrastructure, political decisions and financial capacity. We return to the paradox: the potential for greater access to information has been created by the very technologies which have made it possible, and perhaps even necessary, to restrict that same access.

We should not, however, be pessimistic about this. A longer historical perspective suggests that we are only at an early stage in the revolution which is creating the information society. The computer applications with which much of this chapter has been concerned are, for the most part, less than a decade old as practical working systems. The number of people with some sort of access to networks, and the skills to take advantage of that access, is increasing all the time. The changing balance between the public and private domains has not yet settled into equilibrium or consensus. The political debate which will eventually determine its outcome has barely begun, and has largely concentrated on the single issue of free public library services. We can still hope that the debate will happen, and that there will be a full consideration of the implications of providing, or not providing, effective information services in every sector of society and the economy. Past experience suggests that some time will pass, even at the present rate of technological change, before that debate is fully iterated and resolved.

In the meanwhile, the issues which the debate will address are real, and have real consequences. As information access becomes both easier and more difficult, our dependence on it increases. The overt connection between the value and the cost of information, and the ability to cost service provision as well as to valorize the information itself, is disempowering those with limited economic resources just as the increased use of networks is disempowering those with limited technical resources. Simultaneously, individuals, organizations and states which possess both wealth and skill are accumulating the potential to control information for their own advantage and to deny it to others. These are the central political issues of the information society. They will be considered in Chapter 5 and Chapter 6, as we explore how individuals and governments, and the communities which individuals constitute and governments control, are being changed by the power of information.

5

THE POLITICAL DIMENSION

I Information rich and information poor

It has been argued in Chapter 3 and Chapter 4 that information technology has both facilitated and inhibited access to information. On the one hand, it has greatly increased the ease of storing, sorting and retrieving data; on the other, it has increased the cost of doing so and made that cost more easily quantifiable. By interposing a complex technology with an expensive infrastructure between information and its potential users, it has introduced a new obstacle in the chain of supply. In a later part of this chapter, we shall explore this at the level of information supply to individuals, but it is perhaps most starkly illustrated by considering these issues in the context of states, and, in particular, the nations of the Third World and eastern Europe. This exploration must, however, begin with some more general considerations, for in Chapters 3 and 4 we have assumed that information has an economic or fiscal value. The time has now come to attempt a closer definition of that concept.

THE VALUE OF INFORMATION

Information is a commodity, which is bought and sold. However difficult it may be to define how it acquires value, the fact of the commodification of information cannot be denied. So far, however, we have largely dealt with the financial aspects of the supply of information rather than the value of the information itself.

Books, journals and computer software have a price attached to them at which they are bought and sold. We can assign costs to the construction and maintenance of telecommunications networks, computer hardware, and so on. We can calculate the cost of processing information, in terms of the time involved in obtaining, recording and retrieving it, a cost which would normally be a combination of paying for the time of those involved and the cost of the materials, equipment and consumables they use. None of this, however, really addresses the question of the value – if any – which can be assigned to information.

The problem lies in part in the definition of information itself. Dictionary definitions typically suggest that it is a sub-set of knowledge acquired, deliberately or accidentally, by study or experience. For some purposes, this is adequate: information is simply a part of the total stock of human knowledge. We can, however, take the matter a little further. The transformation of knowledge into information – the systematization of what is known – can be argued to depend on our ability to record knowledge, because the process of recording implies a process of selection. The earliest human records, briefly discussed in Chapter 1, did not represent the total stock of knowledge of palaeolithic man or the ancient Babylonians, but rather that part of the knowledge store that they deemed worthy of recording or necessary to record. Information then is inseparable from our ability to record it.

It does not follow from this, however, that information is inseparable from the medium on which the record is made. On the contrary, one of the characteristics of information is that it can be transferred between media without any significant loss of content. A hand-written sentence might subsequently be typed, word-processed, printed, photocopied and so on, while retaining an unchanged information content. If we add this separability from a medium to inseparability from a recording system of some kind, we arrive at a definition of information as a sub-set of knowledge which is recorded in some symbolic form.

It is in this state, when it is independent of its medium of storage, transmission and retrieval, that we must assign a value to information, for it is only in this state that it has a separate existence. Economists and information scientists (principally the latter), who have addressed this issue are generally agreed that the user rather than the producer determines the value of information, as opposed to its cost. The supplier, the publisher or the bookseller fixes the cost of a book; the value of the information that it contains is a matter for the judgment of the purchaser or the end-user. The value of information, therefore, is an uncertain concept, which cannot easily be quantified. Its value will be perceived differently by different people and perhaps even by the same person depending on the circumstances of time, place and context.

The variability of the value of information – determined by the consumer rather than the producer – is compounded by the fact that its value can be argued to increase as it becomes more common. This apparent paradox – that information, unlike many commodities, has no scarcity value – reflects the origin of information as a sub-set of knowledge. What users are seeking is the sub-set that best meets their needs. Up to the point at which the sub-set is optimized, each additional piece of information increases the value of all those that have already been acquired. Even beyond that point, there may continue to be some accumulation of value, although at a lesser rate, until the point is reached at which there is so much information that it is no longer possible effectively to use it. This is the point of *information overload*, an increasingly common phenomenon in advanced information societies.

The value of information is not intrinsic to the information itself; it depends on its suitability and availability. While it is impossible to assign an absolute value to any given piece of information, it is clear that for the individual user such a value can be assigned. This may be economic, but it may equally be social or cultural. The issue is how much money the end-user is prepared, directly or indirectly, to pay to acquire the information: that ultimately is the measure of its value. Some information, however, may be regarded as a public good; public health information, for example, is supplied by governments and other authorities free of charge (or rather is paid for out of general taxation). Some information may be freely provided as a form of advertising; hence the airline or railway timetables that appear on Websites and elsewhere to encourage potential customers to buy the services being offered. Some information may clearly be a private good to be bought and sold by individuals for their own benefit, as when marketing information is sold to the suppliers of goods and services. A particular piece of information may actually change from private to public good or *vice versa* according to context.

If it is accepted that information has a value, and that this is no mere abstraction, it follows that there can be circumstances in which the absence of information is disadvantageous. In such circumstances, a person or organization (or even a country or its government) is disadvantaged because of what is not known but could be known. The uninformed or under-informed person or organization then becomes a buyer in the information marketplace, provided that the information is available and that they have the resources to acquire it. This does not conflict with the concept that the value of information is determined by the end-user; indeed, it tends to reinforce it, since it is the market that provides a context in which a buyer can determine what is regarded as a fair (or at least acceptable) price.

Against this background (which is no more than a summary of one of the most complex topics in information science), we can understand the concepts of information wealth and poverty, which in turn underpin one of the most important political issues of the information society: who obtains, and who is excluded from, whatever benefits it may have to offer.

INFORMATION IN DEVELOPING COUNTRIES:
AN ISSUE DEFINED

The value of information is not intrinsic, but lies in the uses to which it can be put. From these uses, advantages can be derived that are beneficial to the 'owner' of the information and which would not have been attainable without it. If access to information is controlled, whether fiscally or politically, the potential benefits of possessing it will be lost by those to whom it is denied. These propositions underpin the concepts of 'information wealth' and 'information poverty' and their relationship to economic development.

The furtherance of economic development lies at the heart of national policy-making in all countries, whether industrialized or developing. In broad terms, it suggests the implementation of a planned series of actions leading towards the creation of an infrastructure which will support, in the long term, sustained economic activity and therefore all the other activities which that allows. Such a programme has to be designed and monitored, but it must also be sufficiently flexible to allow the design to be modified in the light of continuous analysis of the monitoring. In other words, the term 'development' implies a dynamic process, a process of change that is not random but planned, and which is aimed at achieving predetermined objectives. The long-term objectives of development are, however, not only economic, for there are also social benefits, improvements to the quality of life. The dynamic of development therefore, is directed not simply towards economic growth – increases in GNP, per capita output, and similar measures of economic success – but also towards less tangible benefits, such as good housing, generally accessible medical services, and an efficient service sector.

The role of the state in this process can vary. In most western countries, it is now largely confined to setting broad targets, such as inflation rates, money supply, levels of unemployment and similar macroeconomic measures. In almost all developing countries, however, the planning process is embodied in a national plan, usually based on a five-year cycle. Within such a plan, the limited resources at the command of the country are directed towards strategic objectives which have been identified as national priorities. Where there is a significant private sector in the economy, it is expected that it too will follow along the broad lines suggested by the national plan, assisted and encouraged by incentives which might take the form of relief from taxation, public investment or support for training.

If it is true that the possession of information is advantageous to the possessor, and its absence is a disadvantage, then it would seem to follow that information is essential to this developmental process. This assumption needs to be examined, and, if it is valid, must lead into a consideration of how far developing countries actually have the infrastructure needed for the provision of effective information services.

The relationship between information and development appears to be close. If, for example, we look at the most successful Asian economies − Japan, Singapore and Korea − we find that they are indeed countries in which economic and scientific information are widely and easily available. In all three, information technology has been developed and exploited to a high level of sophistication. This has led not just to the more effective management of enterprises and institutions, although that has been an important factor, but also to major structural changes in economic activities.

More widespread benefits have accrued because the key role of information in the newly industrialized countries (NICs) has not been limited to the use of information technology in government and business. It has also been critical in the development of new products, in the redesign of existing products and in the creation of new systems for the manufacturing and distribution of goods. Information systems also support the vital service sectors, such as banking, insurance, transport and the media. In other words, while the availability of scientific and technological information has been the necessary foundation for the development of science-based industries, the extended use of information technology has been necessary to create the wider infrastructure within which those industries operate. The comparative success of the information-rich economies, and the comparative weakness of those that are comparatively information poor, is in itself an argument for the importance of information.

In many ways, the NICs of south-east and east Asia are more comparable to the West than they are to other Asian countries. Indeed, two of them – Japan and Singapore – have, in some respects, gone further than the West in exploiting information technology in business and industry and using the facilities which it offers in daily life. Japan, in particular, has developed a vast manufacturing sector of which information technology is an integral part, both as a tool and as a product. Japanese industry makes widespread use of robotics and computer-controlled manufacturing systems (as well as conventional business systems), but the production of information technology hardware is itself a major element in the Japanese industrial economy. Singapore has developed along different lines, using the communications capacity of information technology to turn itself, despite its small size and comparative geographical isolation from other major centres of commerce and industry, into a financial centre of global importance. In both countries, there are, of course, many factors at work other than the use of information technology, but it is, nevertheless, instructive that their respective governments have encouraged the development of the information industry. As a result, they successfully compete even with those western countries which also have advanced information-dependent economies.

The material success of these countries extends beyond the purely economic sector. Social development, such as housing, welfare and medical services, and education, is possible only when there is a sound economic base which can generate the revenue needed to fund these activities. In both Singapore and Japan, the economic success built on the exploitation of information technology has been used to support social development, although in different ways. Singapore, a small, tightly controlled and highly centralized state, has managed to provide a high standard of living for virtually all of its citizens, although some would argue that this has been achieved at the cost of social and political diversity. It is interesting to compare Singapore with Hong Kong in this respect, despite the profound differences in their respective political situations.

Hong Kong, perhaps to an even greater extent than Singapore, has become a global financial centre. Historically a great trading centre, it has been developed as one of the world's most important banking centres, and has consequently attracted vast investments in the financial services sector. As in Singapore, this has been possible on such a scale only because of the existence of instantaneous worldwide communications systems; these can overcome the barriers of distance and time zones which divide Hong Kong from western Europe and North America where its competitors and trading partners are, for the most part, to be found. Under British rule, however, Hong Kong, unlike Singapore, did not build a new social structure on the back of its information-technology driven economic structure. It adhered, perhaps more strictly than anywhere else in the world, to a traditional free market economy. As a result, social development was slow and patchy, and there is a sharp contrast between wealth and poverty which is certainly more apparent than in Singapore. Hong Kong is also unlike Singapore in having a substantial manufacturing sector, but, in contrast to Japan, this sector has not, in general, benefited from the information technology revolution. The ready availability of cheap labour has allowed Hong Kong's manufacturing enterprises to retain traditional practices, which are labour intensive rather than technology based.[1]

These examples suggest that information technology applications can be very diverse, and that both the causes and the consequences of the diversity can be political as well as economic. Singapore, Japan and Hong Kong have all, in different ways, and with different results, exploited information technology in their economic development. Each of them could be argued to be an example of an 'information society'. Each of them, however, also illustrates some of the problems that such societies can generate: uniformity and suppression of dissent to achieve economic success in Singapore; rigid social conformity in Japan; exploitation of the workforce and laggardly social development in Hong Kong.

The perception that the economic success of these advanced Asian economies is information-based is widespread, and it is a perception which is shared in the region itself. Another of the economies of east Asia exemplifies this. Korea was one of the pioneers in implementing a national plan to provide centrally resourced information services to support science-based industry. The lesson has been learned elsewhere in Asia. In Indonesia, for example, the development of information and even library services has been incorporated into national planning, and has received considerable support from the World Bank and the Asia Development Bank.

The mere existence of an information service sector does not, however, guarantee success. Both India and Pakistan, for example, have for many years had scientific information centres similar to that in Korea. Neither INSDOC (Indian Scientific Documentation Centre) nor PASTIC (Pakistan Scientific and Technical Information Centre) have had the effect that was intended on their respective economies, although both provide

---

[1] At the time of writing (August 1997), it is not possible to predict the effects of the Chinese reoccupation of the former colony. Early indications, however, suggest that the economy is sufficiently robust for its continuation in its present form to be likely.

modestly useful information services and document delivery services to scientists in universities and in industry. What is lacking are the resources which only come when there is the political will to support such services. There seems to be little of that recognition of their importance which, alone, would ensure the sustenance of a political initiative. The resources themselves, moreover, can only be found when the economy is successful enough to generate them, and that, in turn, requires a strong infusion of information services, skills and technology. When the economy does begin to take off, the secondary sectors also need information for their effective evolution and operation. This is, perhaps, most obvious in the educational field, where even the most elementary level needs some library facilities for teachers, even if not for the students. Indeed, it might be argued that information is at least as vital in the secondary sectors of the economy as it is in the primary wealth-producing sectors. In some countries, this is indeed recognized. Even in China, for example, with a tradition of centralization which goes back for centuries before the Communist revolution of 1949, it is now acknowledged that market information which will help to sell products is at least as important as the technical information which will help to produce them.

These arguments do not only apply in the industrial and services sectors. They apply to agriculture, which is the most basic industry for many countries in Asia, Africa and Latin America. Scientific agriculture, seeking to maximize crop yields, to eliminate disease and to preserve the quality of the land for future generations, is dependent upon the knowledge of the scientists, and hence on the information sources to which they need access. Agricultural development cannot be achieved without the effective exploitation of information, although, as in other sectors, political, economic and cultural factors can intervene to prevent the effective use of information even when it is theoretically available.

The need for information as a part of the process of development seems to be well established and is coming to be well recognized. Let us turn now to the question of how that information is to be provided. Superficially, the answers are very simple. All that is needed are good libraries, good communications systems and an adequate supply of trained personnel. Those simplicities are not quite so easily realized in practice, and need to be considered in more detail. Such consideration will bring us closer to the central issue of information provision in developing countries, and hence of the relationship between information provision and social and economic development.

WEALTH AND POVERTY:
INFORMATION AND ECONOMIC DEVELOPMENT

The phrases 'information rich' and 'information poor' need to be more precisely defined if this point is to be developed. 'Information rich' is taken to mean a country, an organization or an individual with the information which is needed to carry out the task in hand. 'Information poor' can then be defined in opposite and negative terms to describe those who lack that information. We must, however, be careful not to equate information wealth and information poverty with particular kinds of information supplied through particular media or institutions. The farmer who knows the annual patterns of the weather and of the water level in the river which irrigates his land may have sufficient information to grow an adequate crop to feed his family. In that sense he is information rich. The farmer's information wealth, however, is only comparative. If he wishes to increase the yield of his land and grow cash crops, or if he wishes to change crops, or if he wishes in any way to modify the traditional patterns to which he works, then he will need to enrich his information resources. If he cannot, he becomes a victim of information poverty, and will suffer in comparison with those who do have access to information.

This homely example can usefully be pursued a little further, for it opens up a number of important themes. It can be argued that the farmer who wants to change traditional patterns of work has already obtained information beyond that which he needed in order to work in the traditional way. He knows that change is possible. He may have observed it on his neighbour's land. He may have heard about it on the radio, or seen programmes about it on television. He may have been told about it by an agricultural advisor employed by the government or by some other agency. The intermediary is irrelevant; what is important is that the farmer has acquired information. Without that, he would not have known that change was possible. Having obtained it, he can – perhaps with more help and advice – begin to evaluate it and consider whether the change is desirable or necessary. In order to make changes, he needs yet more information, about how to achieve new patterns of production and work. Most obviously, he will need to know about seeds and chemicals. He may need to know about machinery and equipment. At a secondary level, however, he will also need information: about sources of supply of these items, and almost certainly about how he can obtain the money that will be necessary to provide the initial capital for his new enterprise.

This sequence of events can be considered as a possible model for the connection between information provision and the development process. Our farmer was originally self-sustaining, and needed only that information which he had obtained when he first began to work, almost certainly orally, and probably from within the family. He then became aware of the possibility of change. This awareness arose out of his access to sources of information. He then took a decision to make changes. His next step was to seek further information about how to implement this decision, and almost immediately he was seeking information about services as well as goods. To improve his economic status, he could no longer confine his activities to one sector of the economy, but had to have access to others. At each stage, information was the catalyst that first created awareness, and then facilitated decision-making and implementation.

Another way of expressing this is to say that the farmer recognized that his information wealth was only superficial; when he recognized the possibility of change, he was also recognizing the need to remedy his relative information poverty. The details of this model may not be universal, and perhaps few, if any, of those who conform to it would recognize it as a description of what they are doing, but it is, nevertheless, broadly accurate and widely applicable. As more information is acquired, more becomes necessary to implement the decisions based on the analysis of newly acquired information. The process is cyclical as well as progressive. It is a model which combines all the essential features of awareness of the need for information and access to appropriate sources and systems.

INFORMATION DELIVERY SYSTEMS: SOME CONTRASTS

The appropriateness of the information delivery systems is particularly important in this context. In Chapter 2, we considered development of the many ways in which information can now be delivered to end-users, and throughout Chapters 3 and 4 we have been considering various aspects of the delivery mechanisms. We normally receive information by hearing it or by seeing it, but, as we have seen, these simple sensory functions can be addressed in many different ways. We may hear information on a one-to-one basis, or in a group, or in a public speech; we may hear it privately from someone in another location through a telephone or a two-way radio; we may hear it through a public medium such as broadcast radio, or prerecorded audio tape. Some of these media may be partly visual, like the public speech. Other media are heavily dependent on visual impact, most obviously television, video and cinema, and, of course, the display screen of a computer. A particular piece of information can be transmitted by any or all of these methods, although some are more effective than others in particular circumstances. The choice of medium is critical in ensuring that the message which it conveys reaches its intended recipient and can be effectively exploited when it is received.

The effectiveness of the information transfer process depends on the effectiveness of the communication system through which the transfer is to take place, and that, in turn, depends on whether the target audience has access to the medium and can understand the message it conveys. Our farmer may be illiterate, but an illiterate person can absorb information through television or some other aural or visual medium. At a macro-level, however, the very technologies that have made the information transfer process so much more effective, have, as has already been argued, emphasized and perhaps increased the differences between the information rich and the information poor.

Technology is beginning to provide some of the answers to some of the problems it has created. The advent of CD-ROM means that online access is no longer the only way into complex databases. As we have seen, although the CD-ROM is inevitably a little less current than the database of which it is a copy, it is both easier to use and more economical to produce than its printed equivalent, and can, of course, be updated rather than merely supplemented at regular intervals. The hardware needed for access to CD-ROMs is comparatively inexpensive, and is both cheap and easy to maintain compared with the high capital and running costs of online access. CD-ROM has had the effect of removing the telecommunications element from the information technology equation. This is of the utmost importance in developing countries, where the telecommunications infrastructure is often weak, and the technology for transmitting digitized data often does not exist.

Even so, it is clear that the most economically successful of the developing countries have been those which have invested most heavily and most expertly in the infrastructure of information technology, and in particular in the development of effective telecommunications systems for networking. The second-line Asian economies – Indonesia, Thailand, Malaysia and the Philippines – are rapidly following the examples of Singapore, Korea, Hong Kong and Japan, and indeed the western countries, in seeking to develop information and telecommunications systems as a high priority. Such developments will, however, take time, and their very cost means that their availability will be limited. It is not difficult to envisage a situation in which an NIC is information rich at the national level, but contains large pockets of information poverty, which might even encompass the majority of the population. In some countries in Asia and in Latin America this danger has already been realized.

An associated danger is that more traditional means of access to information will be neglected. This manifests itself in several ways, of which two are particularly important. First, as we have suggested in Chapter 3, the greater part of the world's information resources takes the form of print-on-paper, which is still the most common medium of information dissemination. It follows, therefore, that a well-organized and properly skilled publishing industry, an efficient book trade, and well-stocked and well-managed libraries, remain the key elements in any nation's information infrastructure, and underpin its formal education system.

Secondly, it should be remembered that beyond the small world of the professional users of information – scientists, managers, policy-makers – the most important information and communication medium is not the computer but broadcasting, and in particular television. This is true in the industrialized world, but perhaps the phenomenon is even more obvious in the developing countries. Television overcomes problems of illiteracy, and even of imperfect knowledge of language itself, by exploiting visual images. Although primarily a medium of entertainment, it can and does inform, and, in countries where it is strictly state-controlled, television can be used very effectively for that purpose. Such use can, of course, take the form of propaganda, and it is perhaps inevitable that it should do so. There are, however, many more positive uses. In Pakistan, for example, television, radio and pre-recorded taped material have been used very effectively for many years by the Allama Iqbal Open University, perhaps the most successful of several attempts to provide such an institution in a developing country.

Books and television continue to be the most effective of educational and informational media, despite the apparent predominance of the computer. In other words, we need to maintain and to develop the infrastructure needed for both printed and the broadcast media if we are to sustain a full range of information resources for developmental activities. There is a real problem here. We must never fall into the error of assuming that information can only be provided if we have access to computer-based information systems. Nevertheless, such systems do play a key role in making information available in the industrialized countries, and the evidence that this is economically significant is overwhelming. This suggests the depressing conclusion that the gap between information wealth and information poverty is widening rather than narrowing as the information infrastructure in the industrialized countries leaps even further ahead of that elsewhere.

NORTH AND SOUTH: THE WORLD PUBLISHING INDUSTRY

It is a conclusion that is supported by considering other aspects of economic development in many parts of the world. The industrialized countries themselves encountered major economic difficulties in the late 1980s and early 1990s, and this inevitably had effects on their relations with the developing countries. The north–south divide, between the rich industrialized north and the poor agricultural south, is more marked than ever. As it widens, it becomes more difficult to cross. This phenomenon is as marked in the information sector as it is in other areas of social and economic activity. The point can be illustrated by considering the publishing industry.

During two centuries of expansion outside Europe, the British carried the English language to every continent. British power and influence was so pervasive that English became the international language of commerce, diplomacy and science, and has essentially retained that position long after Britain's withdrawal from empire. As a result, international publishing is dominated by books in English, of which the majority, as we saw in Chapter 3, are now published in the USA, although the UK is the source of a sizeable minority. English therefore remains the language of business, government and education in many countries in Asia and Africa, and in some countries, such as Nigeria and India, for example, English is, in effect, the only common language in which people from different tribal or cultural groups can communicate.

For British and American publishers this is a great boon, for it means that their markets are global. Another consequence, however, is that the book trade is weak in many of the consumer countries. Buying western books means paying western prices, and, moreover, paying those prices in hard currency. This, in itself, is a major obstacle to educational development. Libraries in many Asian and African countries, including some which are certainly not at the lowest levels of poverty such as Kenya or India, are able to spend only a fraction of what they need to maintain anything like a reasonable collection of materials. This has been, and continues to be, a serious hindrance to the development of secondary and tertiary education and of academic and industrial research.

The alternative is the development of indigenous publishing, but this too has proved difficult. With the exception of India, there is no English-speaking developing country or NIC with a sufficiently large domestic base to support a flourishing publishing industry. Where such industries have developed, it has generally been for one of two reasons. There are those countries where there is a genuine competitor to English as the common language, such as Malaysia where Bahasa publishing flourishes and successive governments have encouraged its development as a national cultural policy. There are also countries, such as Kenya, Malawi and Zambia, where state or semi-state publishing houses produce primary- and secondary-level educational textbooks in local languages. In both cases, however, the linguistic base of the industry effectively bars it from seeking global markets, and is a disincentive to local authors who seek a readership beyond the boundaries of their own country. As a result, even those countries which have begun to develop publishing industries are still dependent on imports for higher-level books, and are unable to attract even their own native authors into publishing locally in world languages.

The continued dominance of English-language publishing by the British and American publishers and distributors, able to exploit huge domestic markets and global sales organizations, exemplifies the problem of the information poor of the south. The southern countries are forced to compete in an arena dominated by northern countries whose inherent economic strength rests on an infrastructure which the south cannot replicate. The creation of new channels of information transfer through new systems of communication has merely exacerbated the situation. Inadequate telecommunications are perhaps the most important technical obstacle. Without better connections, there can be no online access to the Internet or other online services whether for academic, industrial or commercial purposes. Even fax is difficult. The south is effectively being excluded from the communications revolution, and as scientists and others in the industrialized countries become more reliant on electronic communications, those in the developing world will suffer accordingly.

CD-ROM offers at least a partial solution to this problem, but it is only partial. It does indeed give easy and comparatively cheap access to databases, but most of those available in this format are bibliographic, and assume subsequent access to document delivery services, full-text databases, CD-ROMs, or the World Wide Web, in order to obtain the primary information. Such services are often inadequate in less developed countries, and where they do exist they are expensive. Few developing countries have succeeded in devising infrastructures for interlibrary-lending and document delivery at national level, while to use international services, even when they are accessible, again involves the expenditure of rare hard currency. Only the most favoured institutions are normally able to do this. Consequently, the potential beneficiaries of information in the universities and governments and industrial enterprises of the Third World are all too often deprived of the information that they need for their further development.

The cycle of information poverty, and its consequences, is only too obvious when we consider the gap between the north and the south. It does seem, however, that the cycle can be broken. Malaysia and Indonesia, for example, have apparently begun to do so by exploiting their natural resources to generate the essential hard currency which allows them to buy the tools and expertise that they need for the next stage of development. Thailand is probably moving down the same road although not without much difficulty and economic pain. In all three cases, large and broadly homogeneous populations (although there are minorities, mainly ethnic Chinese, in all of them) have been mobilized to provide the labour which can still, to some extent, compensate for the lack of technology in the early stages of development. Nothing, however, can compensate for inadequate information infrastructures, and in all three countries the development of these infrastructures is now a priority. In this way, they are breaking through into the ranks of the newly industrialized. Although it is extremely difficult to demonstrate the importance of information in this process, the Asian examples suggest that there is a link between development and the existence of an effective information infrastructure. Similar patterns can be discerned elsewhere.

EASTERN EUROPE: A DIFFERENT POVERTY?

A very different form of information poverty exists in eastern Europe. There, it was deliberately created by the totalitarian regimes which prevailed until the end of the 1980s. Some parts of the infrastructure were well developed, but other aspects were inhibited or even forbidden. Television, for example, was a medium of propaganda and entertainment rather than of information, as radio had been before it. It was, therefore, widely available and well resourced. The telecommunications systems, on the other hand, were deliberately underdeveloped, so that there was only limited access even to domestic telephones. International calls, other than through intrusive operators, were normally impossible, and fax facilities were rare. Computers did, of course, exist and were widely used for scientific purposes, but again international communications were all but impossible, and so was access to international databases. This was an information poverty which was deliberately created by the state because of the dangers which it perceived in allowing its citizens easy access to information and communications systems.

Since 1989, much effort and money has been devoted to remedying some of these defects. New telecommunications systems, and the widespread use of information technology, are high on the list of priorities of the new eastern European governments and the western countries and agencies which are supporting their efforts. It is recognized that effective communications are essential if the countries of eastern Europe are to share in the comparative prosperity of the West, even though the strain on the western economies of trying to absorb the East is perhaps damaging the very prosperity in which the East hopes to share. In other ways, however, the eastern countries have indeed entered into the information market-place. In some of them, newspapers now compete with each other for a market share, and operate without many of the legal constraints which formerly prevented the free dissemination of information and opinion about current affairs. Satellite television is widely accessible, and with it the vast range of information and entertainment which it transmits. Book and magazine publishing has also been freed from the constraints of the censor, and books can be produced and imported without restriction. Moreover, unlike the developing countries of the south, the former socialist countries already have the basic industrial and commercial infrastructure within which a book trade and a newspaper industry can develop. The road may be a long one, but the journey has clearly begun.

THE LIMITS OF WEALTH: INFORMATION POVERTY IN THE WEST

It is not only, however, in the developing countries or in the shattered economies of eastern Europe that information poverty is to be found. It is pervasive in the West, either by neglect or by design, although it is of a different order from the information poverty of the Second and Third Worlds. To understand the phenomenon, we have to make a distinction between the absence of information itself and defects in the means of access to it. The difference is fundamental, for while the former may be remediable by comparatively straightforward actions, to remedy the latter is almost always both expensive and complicated.

A simple example will illustrate the point. In Britain and the USA, ignorance of current affairs is widespread. Public opinion polls reveal that even such basic facts as the name of the prime minister or the president are unknown to a significant percentage of the adult population. Slightly more complex enquiries, such as asking respondents to identify the photographs of allegedly well-known public figures, usually yield failure rates in excess of 50%. Pop musicians, television performers and sports personalities are, on the whole, more generally recognized than political leaders. Ignorance of public affairs is not a consequence of lack of opportunity, but of lack of interest. In both the UK and the USA, virtually 100% of the population have access to television, and watch it regularly; radio is equally universal. The names of both countries' national leaders are heard every day on both media, and their faces seen as often on television. Ignorance is deliberate, the result of exercising a choice not to know. The means of remedying the ignorance are, however, at hand; the problem is lack of information, not lack of access.

Where there is defective access, or indeed no access at all, it is altogether more serious. It can exist at many levels. A household does not have access to satellite television channels unless it has the equipment on which it can receive and decode the signal. This may be a matter of choice – a conscious decision not to buy the equipment – or it may be a decision forced on the household by economic circumstances. The example is deliberately chosen as a comparatively trivial one, but the model which it suggests can be applied in more serious cases. The company without access to market information which is known to a competitor is at a disadvantage which may be insuperable. The academic without network access is excluded from discussion lists, access to the Web, and so on. The examples can be multiplied.

More insidious is the deliberate deprivation of information by those who seek to use ignorance as an instrument to achieve their own ends. The example of the controlled media of eastern Europe before 1989 illustrates this. The state effectively prevented information from being circulated unless it was to its own advantage; at other times it circulated misleading or false information, again for its own ends. The use of misinformation and disinformation is considered in more detail in Chapter 6; here, we need only notice its existence. Inhibition of information transfer is not, however, practised only by the state. A salesperson is deliberately selective in the information given to a potential customer; without deviating from the truth in what is said, much can be left unsaid. This is a fundamental technique for salespeople and politicians alike. When one party to a transaction is deprived of information known to the other party, the less well-informed is inevitably the weaker partner. This is not only true in commercial transactions. The social security claimant who knows less about the system than the employee of the benefit agency is disadvantaged in making a case for support. Both consumers and citizens – that is everybody – need information if they are to be on even approximately equal terms with the organizations with which they have to deal.

Once again, we confront the paradox of information technology. On the one hand, the dissemination of information is far easier, and far more pervasive, than ever before. By contrast, the difficulty of accessing the information which can, theoretically, be so widely disseminated, has created information-rich elites, and, consequently, pockets of information poverty. Some of these pockets, as we have seen, contain whole nations and even whole regions of the world. Others are smaller, but membership of them is no less disadvantageous. In the West, the information poor are, in general, those who are also deprived in other ways. Indeed, it is impossible to evade the conclusion that there is a link between lack of information and lack of other forms of social and economic benefit.

Information systems have, generally, been constructed by those who are literate, articulate and well educated. Even using a public teletext service requires some basic information retrieval skills such as an understanding of indexing, and some elementary skills in the interpretation of instructions and the use of equipment. To use the online catalogue in a library or to surf the Web probably requires specific training by demonstration or reading. Accessing a database can be a skilled task, perhaps even needing the intervention of a trained information worker or someone who, although not an information worker, has acquired those particular information retrieval skills. As the system becomes more complex, the need for an intermediary becomes more marked. An inability to understand the potential of the system, or to communicate effectively with those who do, can create information poverty where none should exist. The systems themselves thus place an additional barrier between the information and its potential beneficiary.

The information poor in industrialized countries are generally being deprived of information which is available if only they knew how to gain access to it either directly or by asking those with different skills from their own. Librarians, to their great credit, are increasingly aware of this gap and of the need to cross it. Community information services, genuinely user-friendly public access information systems and the like, are some of the manifestations of this. Other agencies and professionals seem to be somewhat less aware of the problem, or are, perhaps, less willing to address the issues which it raises. In the UK, such documents as Income Tax returns and, most notoriously, the leaflets which allegedly 'explain' social security entitlements, have become legendary for their obscurity. By bad presentation, the state is depriving the citizen of information to which the state itself has determined that the citizen has a right of access. We shall return to this matter in Chapter 6.

Information poverty is a disadvantage when it deprives its victims of information which could be of benefit to them. Such benefits might be financial, professional, social, educational or purely a matter of personal convenience. It takes its place in the cycle of deprivation with other, more tangible, manifestations of poverty. Deprived of essential information, the citizen is deprived of the power of choice, because only informed choice can be rational choice. These consequences are, in many ways, analogous with the consequences of poor information infrastructures in the Third World or in eastern Europe. The information elites of the industrialized world are becoming ever more isolated from the excluded majorities, just as the economic gap between north and south is generally widening. There are, of course, exceptions; individuals can work their way into the elites, just as countries can. Skill acquisition, through education or training, can change the relationship between an individual and the information base of society, just as Indonesia or Thailand can hope to break through the barriers to industrialized status. The obstacles, however, remain, and the rate of enlargement of the elite is still small compared with the number of those excluded.

The relationship between the information rich and the information poor is the central political dilemma of the information society. Access to information has become one of the points of conflict within and between societies, and one of the measures of success and failure. The state has a multi-faceted role; it is, at the same time, the creator, owner and protector of information, but also must try to encompass the interests of both the information rich and the information poor. The next chapter explores various aspects of this dilemma.

6

THE POLITICAL DIMENSION
2 Information, the state and the citizen

The value which can be assigned to information, both directly and indirectly, has done more than simply turn it into a commodity to be traded in the market-place. There is some information which can never be the simple neutral subject of a commercial transaction. Possessing it can bring too many benefits, and not possessing it too many disadvantages, for that to be possible. The creators of information are creating a piece of valuable property, which may be intended for sale, or may be regarded as being too valuable to the creator and possessor to be made available at all. These circumstances have created a complex and sometimes shadowy set of relationships between information itself, its creators, owners and providers, individual consumers or beneficiaries of information, and the apparatus of a state which seeks to regulate these interactions.

THE ROLE OF THE STATE: AN INTRODUCTION

In essence, the state can intervene in four ways between the information owner and the information-seeker. First, it can protect information as a piece of property in which the rights of ownership clearly belong to its legal possessor. This is the function of the law of copyright, and the growing number of associated forms of protection known to lawyers as 'adjacent rights' or, more generally, 'intellectual property'. Secondly, the state can prevent the unauthorized use of information that has been legitimately collected. This is the purpose of the growing body of law concerned with the protection of data, especially data on the personal and financial affairs of individuals. Thirdly, the state can guarantee the right of access to certain categories of information of interest or benefit to its citizens. Freedom of information legislation works in several ways, but is normally concerned primarily with facilitating general access to information of general importance, while ensuring that individuals are aware of, and have some control over, data that concerns them at a personal level. Finally, the state can prevent the dissemination of information. This can be for reasons of security, morality or political expediency, and can be overt or covert; it is, necessarily, the most difficult area to explore.

THE ROLE OF THE STATE:
THE PROTECTION OF INTELLECTUAL PROPERTY

The need to afford some sort of protection to the owners of information was recognized for centuries before the concept would have been expressed in those terms. The distant origins of copyright lie in privileges granted by secular states and ecclesiastical authorities to individual printers and authors, the earliest examples of which are to be found in Italy and France before the end of the fifteenth century. There was a mixture of motives behind these grants. Some were intended to encourage the practitioners of the new and expensive craft of printing, perhaps because it was considered to be socially and culturally useful. Some were intended to control the output of the press by limiting the numbers of printers and thereby making it easier to supervize their activities. In practice, these two approaches to the control and protection of the press became inextricably mixed. Censorship, in some form, was almost universal in early modern Europe, and it was out of the attempts to protect the state from the press that the book trade was able to develop the rights which allowed the state to afford it some protection.

In modern times, two traditions of copyright law have sometimes been identified, although in recent years there has been convergence between them. The British, or common law, tradition, which has been influential in the USA and throughout the English-speaking world, understands copyright as a piece of property, which can be traded like any other commodity. The alternative Roman law tradition, which was first embodied in the *Code Napoléon*, and which influences the legal traditions of southern Europe and the Francophone and Hispanophone countries, regards copyright as a right which essentially belongs to the author, and over which the author retains 'moral rights', or *droit moral*, even after publication. The differences and conflicts between these traditions are not as marked as has sometimes been presented. Although they do indeed represent different approaches to copyright as a concept, by setting commercial property against artistic integrity, the practical results are very similar. In both legal traditions, the primary purpose of copyright law is to ensure that those who are responsible for the creation and publication of a work have a reasonable opportunity to profit from it, and to prevent those who were not involved in the process from benefiting from the labours of others. Copyright law thus operates on two levels. On one level, it protects authors and publishers. It is the legal embodiment of the concept of information as property, and provides a mechanism for preventing the infringement of property rights; if prevention fails, it defines forms of punishment and prescribes penalties. At another level, copyright law regulates the circumstances under which copying and dissemination can legitimately happen.

In practice, copyright normally takes the form of granting absolute protection to a newly created work for a fixed period of time. In many countries, this is now the author's lifetime and 50 years thereafter; in the European Union it is 70 years after death.

During that time, the work can only be reproduced with the permission of the author or the author's representatives. These representatives may be individuals or organizations to whom the rights have been sold or leased by the author. The function of the law in these commercial transactions between author and publisher is to provide the framework within which they can safely be conducted. The law of copyright protects the author's investment of intellectual effort and the publisher's investment of professional skill and risk capital. The same principle is extended to other areas of creative and intellectual activity. The law protects, in various ways, products as diverse as paintings and computer software, or indeed any thing that is derived from the exercise of human imagination and skill. The essence of the law is that the product may be reproduced, or in some cases used, only with the permission of the creator, thus giving that person (or corporate body) the opportunity to recoup their intellectual and perhaps financial investment.

Expressed in that way, the law of intellectual property seems neat and simple. In practice it is neither, partly because different manifestations of such property have to be treated in different ways. These arise from the inherent differences between the communication media which are used for information in different formats. The classic historical model of the copyright in a book has developed because of the printing and publishing process itself, with its heavy front-loaded investment of capital, and the author's partly conflicting desires both to disseminate the work and to protect it against dissemination by others. Illegally reprinting a book, however, is no easy matter, although it does happen, as we shall see. On the other hand, there are now technologies in which ease of copying and transmission are the very core of the information transfer process.

The most obvious of these is computing. The legal protection of computer software is fraught with problems. In current British law, under the Copyright (Computer Software) Amendment Act

(1985) and the Copyright, Designs and Patent Act (1988), the position is that a computer program is as fully protected as if it were any other kind of intellectual property, such as a conventional written work. Similarly, the data stored in a database is protected on exactly the same basis. In practice, this can lead to many complications. When a customer buys a copy of a computer program, such as a word-processing package, what is acquired is the right to use that copy only. The purchaser does not, for example, have the right to make a second copy of the program to use simultaneously on another computer. An important principle is embodied in this prohibition; the purchaser would not necessarily obtain direct financial benefit from the making of a second copy for personal use, but the owner of the rights in the program suffers the loss incurred by not selling a second copy. In fact, it is extremely difficult for the publishers of software to prevent such copying by private individuals, and they tend to concentrate their efforts on preventing illegal commercial exploitation of their products by the production and sale of pirated copies on a large scale. In addition, many software houses will grant so-called 'site licences', under which institutional purchasers (such as universities or companies) pay for the right to make a specified number of copies of a particular program for use on their premises for specific purposes or to run the software or database on their own network for internal use at a specified number of workstations. This is an invaluable compromise between unenforceable prohibitions and uncontrolled infringement of rights.

Intellectual property law is intended to be of benefit to both the creators and the users of information, by ensuring that the information market-place has a commercially sound basis. It achieves this by protecting the investment of the author and the publisher in the creation of the work and in its multiplication in a marketable format. Because the publisher acquires an effective monopoly of a particular work, it is possible to take the financial risk involved in making it available for sale and also to pay the author for the right to do so. The British tradition of regarding copyright as a commercial matter is exemplified in this approach. On the other hand, copyright and other intellectual property rights can sometimes operate to the apparent disadvantage of the user, and there is a need to maintain a balance between the interests of producers and those of the consumers whose demand creates the market which gives the product its commercial value in the first place. Two examples will illustrate this.

First, the law regulates the extent of photocopying of published material. Theoretically, all photocopying of copyright material is a breach of the general principle of copyright protection. In practice, technological developments have forced legislators to take a less extreme position. The concept of 'fair dealing', which is now embodied in the law in most industrialized countries, makes provision for limited amounts of photocopying for non-commercial purposes. These include private study, and, in certain circumstances, educational use. The law may also make provision (as the 1988 British law does) for licensing arrangements which facilitate the making of multiple photocopies for legitimate purposes, while ensuring that the copyright owners receive some financial compensation for the notional loss of sales which this entails.

There are, however, further issues to be considered. In the academic world, where most of the copying under the 'fair dealing' rules takes place, the principal concern is with copying papers in journals. When the fair dealing rules were first evolved in the late 1950s, it was argued that the publishers of such journals did not, in practice, suffer any loss by allowing limited copying for personal use, since it was considered to be highly improbable that the person making the copy would subscribe to the journal if copying were not permitted. The development of centralized document delivery services, however, has dealt a serious blow to this argument. Licensing arrangements may protect the publishers to some extent, and document delivery services are expected to be vigilant in upholding both the law in general and the fair dealing rules in particular, but lapses are inevitable. The publishers' interests were damaged by conventional, photocopy-based, document delivery services. Even greater damage is possible from network transmission of digitized images of documents, when the line between printed and electronic publication is no longer so clearly drawn.

It would be difficult to disprove the publishers' contention that large-scale document delivery services have had a deleterious effect on sales, although their development has also coincided with a period of rising journal prices, an increased number of journal titles and a decline in the purchasing power of library budgets. The inevitable consequence has been to set up a vicious circle in which the easy availability of low-price document delivery services results in libraries cancelling subscriptions to periodicals which can be accessed through those services. As a result, the publishers must decrease the print run of the journal and increase its price, causing further loss of subscriptions and further price rises. This chain of events is already well advanced, and is one of the reasons why there is so much interest in the potential of the electronic journal, as was suggested in Chapter 4. The potential for conflict between the needs of users and their ability to pay for information, on the one hand, and, on the other hand, the need for information providers to make a reasonable profit in order to sustain their continued activities, is only too clear. Publishers and information service providers (especially university libraries) are now recognizing the need to work together to resolve this conflict.

The conflict is essentially economic, but the second example of the difficulties that can arise out of copyright law has more overt cultural and educational implications. As we have suggested in Chapters 3 and 5, the information market-place is dominated by producers based in industrialized countries. More specifically, world publishing is dominated by the British and American publishers of books in the English language, who have an almost complete monopoly of high level publishing in STM and academic publishing. The books and journals which they produce are necessarily expensive, sometimes even by western standards. Consequently, less developed countries have the utmost difficulty in obtaining such material. It is one of the more obvious ways in which cash poverty leads directly to information poverty. Publishers are not in business as aid agencies, yet they do have some self-interest in trying to help the developing world to solve this dilemma. Again, technology lies at the root of the problem. It is often cheaper to make a photocopy of a book than it is to buy a copy of the book itself. For those who are remote from any likelihood of detection or punishment, the temptation may be irresistible. As with the photocopying of journal articles, however, the problem is not a serious one until it begins to interfere with legitimate trade. This happens if the illicit copies of a book are sold to those who would otherwise buy the original; the owner of the intellectual property is then clearly being deprived of rewards legitimated by the law.

Photocopying is a very crude and clumsy technology for mass copying for commercial purposes. There is, however, a far greater danger. Modern printing technology is also based on photographic systems. Photolithography, the system now in common use, prints images from photographic plates which are both simple and relatively cheap to make. It is possible to make a plate from the page of a printed book without much greater difficulty than that involved in photocopying the same page. As an alternative, a copy of the book can be digitized by a scanning device, and the output used to generate plates. From these plates, the book can then be reproduced on a printing press, and will appear to be identical with the original. If identical paper is used, and an identical binding made, the deception will be complete. Such piracy (as this form of theft is rather romantically known) is common in some parts of the world; in some NICs it represents a substantial part of the work of sophisticated printing industries. For the western publishers, piracy is a very serious problem. The success of the piratical reprints of English-language books of all kinds, from popular fiction to STM monographs, demonstrates the existence of a market for such books. Yet it is one which the original publishers themselves cannot aspire to reach; their prices are too high, for they are locked into the high-cost economics which dominate the book production industry in the industrialized world. Moreover, western governments have not been entirely unsympathetic to the complaints of the governments of developing countries that the high prices of essential educational and scientific books is actually hindering development by inhibiting education and research. It was out of such arguments that the idea was developed of licensing reprints in developing countries for domestic use in those countries.

Since the late nineteenth century, copyright law, and indeed all law relating to intellectual property, has been steadily internationalized. Ideas are no respecters of international political boundaries, and the books and other information media which carry them are just as difficult to restrict. The basic principle of international copyright law is very simple: all books, regardless of their 'national' origin, are fully protected in any country as if they had originated there. The practice is embodied in two major conventions which are the basis of international copyright law. These are the Berne Convention, originally signed in 1886 but subsequently much modified, and the Universal Copyright Convention (UCC), signed in 1952 and, like Berne, subject to subsequent modifications. Although the two conventions have some important differences of approach, in fact most countries are signatories of both, and both incorporate the essential principle of reciprocity, Berne somewhat more strictly than UCC. It was in revising the Berne Convention in the late 1960s and early 1970s that the problem of book availability in the developing countries was firmly addressed.

The technical and legal details need not concern us. The

important point is that the Paris Act (sometimes referred to as the 'Paris Amendments') modified the Berne Convention by introducing the principle that developing countries should have special privileges and rights in relation to the reprinting of copyright materials needed for educational and developmental purposes. In essence, a publisher in a developing country can apply to a western publisher for a licence to reprint a title in which that publisher holds the rights, and the western publisher is obliged to grant the licence without charge. There are, however, two essential conditions: the reprint is for domestic use in the producer country and not for export, and the work must be intended for educational purposes. In other words, the Paris Act was an attempt to solve the problem of the supply of essential, but necessarily very expensive, western books to the developing world. There is some evidence that it has indeed had this effect.

These two examples of the workings of copyright law – the photocopying of journal articles and the reprinting of western books elsewhere in the world – illustrate how it can inhibit the dissemination of information. This inhibition is not, of course, accidental. The whole point of protecting intellectual property of any kind is to ensure that it is disseminated in a way which benefits its creators and protects their interests. The difficulties arise when this legitimate desire to protect property comes into conflict with the equally legitimate needs of potential beneficiaries. The decisions to be taken in resolving this conflict are political rather than professional. The protection afforded by patents, for example, is, for all practical purposes, absolute. Like computer software, the use of a patent may be licensed to named producers (as often happens in the pharmaceutical industry, for example) but the rights clearly remain with their original owner, or, in rare cases, outright purchaser.

Intellectual property law is, in effect, the regulator of the information market-place, determining the conditions under which trading is conducted there. Like any regulatory mechanism, it is both inhibitory and permissive. It is generally, however, intended to stimulate the information transfer process by protecting the financial and intellectual interests of those who have created information products of any kind. The very concept is an extension beyond the usual limits of the law of property, where the state normally intervenes only to protect the owner against infringements of what is rightfully owned. In dealing with intellectual property, the law makes the assumption, which we have detected elsewhere, that information is so important that its owners and those responsible for its commercial dissemination must be afforded some additional protection. Originally this concept was, perhaps, not dissimilar from the 'cultural' case for regulating book prices discussed in Chapter 4.

From the middle of the eighteenth century onwards, authors were increasingly aware of their 'rights' and of their role in the creation of commercially valuable products. Gradually, these rights were recognized by the law and incorporated into it. Different traditions produced different results. In Britain, from 1842 to 1988, the law essentially recognized the author as a partner in a series of commercial transactions; French law (and the American Constitution) broadened this understanding to include the author's 'moral right' to protect the artistic integrity of the work. In 1988, this concept was at last incorporated into British law. Authors now retain moral rights in the work, and can forbid it to be used or altered in ways of which they do not approve. The law, like the society of which it is a product, sees artistic and literary works, and especially perhaps books, as being, in some ill-defined but nevertheless broadly accepted way, 'different'.

THE ROLE OF THE STATE:
DATA PROTECTION AND PERSONAL PRIVACY

It could be argued that there is a fundamental ambiguity in the modern approach to intellectual property law: on the one hand it seeks to facilitate the operation of the market-place, while, on the other, it seeks to protect the integrity of some of the products made for that market-place. A similar ambiguity, resulting perhaps from the sheer complexity of the subject, can be seen when we turn to a more contentious subject: the state's role in the storage, use and regulation of personal data.

The protection of personal data is not a new issue, but it is one which, in its contemporary form, is closely linked to the evolution of computing and the ever-increasing use of the computer by governments, institutions and businesses. Vast quantities of data are collected for perfectly legitimate purposes. In an industrialized country, for example, various agencies of the state hold information about the nationality, age, marital status, family circumstances, income, health and place of residence of individuals. These are collected for such purposes as assessing and collecting taxes, issuing passports, ensuring the right to vote, providing welfare benefits and recording the obligation to undertake such duties as serving on a jury or performing a period of compulsory military service. In other words, the state collects the information which is needed to ensure that its citizens fulfil their obligations and receive their entitlements. No modern state could function without such information. Computers have transformed the efficiency and comprehensiveness of the processes of collecting, sorting and using the data, but not its fundamental purpose.

It is not, however, only governments which hold information about individuals. A great deal is held by other public or semi-public bodies. Local or regional governments (depending upon the constitutional arrangements in force in particular countries) may hold some or all of the information also held by central governments. In the USA, for example, some states have their own income taxes, which means that they, as well as the federal government, hold information relating to personal and corporate incomes. In Britain, information about the value of property is held by local authorities for whom it is the basis of their calculation of the tax obligations of residents and property owners. However, information is also held by many non-governmental public sector bodies, such as schools, universities and hospitals and other health-care agencies. Unlike central and local government, these bodies are not directly accountable through a democratically elected representative body to those about whom the information is held.

In the private sector, there is no visible accountability, and yet the amount of information held is vast. It includes some which is of great personal sensitivity, such as financial data, data which record personal expenditure, travel arrangements and similar private activities. The largest sets of these records are, in a sense, created accidentally. Credit-card transactions are usually automated from the moment they take place, through online links to the card-issuer's computer which checks the state of the cardholder's account. Even when the actual transaction is manual, the credit company will eventually create a computer-held record which will calculate interest payments, issue invoices, record payments, and so on. All this is innocuous, and beneficial to the user of the service that the company provides. The records that are created, however, have a vast potential for misuse because of the records of expenditure which they create. Moreover, because credit transactions have become such an important element in the pattern of personal expenditure in most industrialized countries, agencies have been established which collect such data and use it to establish a credit rating for individuals. On this basis, a person may be refused further credit, not merely by a company with which he or she already has an account, but by another agency for a quite different purpose. Credit rating agencies are regulated, and banks and other financial institutions are bound by legal as well as professional requirements of secrecy and confidentiality, Nevertheless, there is a growing body of evidence of abuse of the credit rating system, as well as inevitable errors which can seriously disadvantage an individual or even devastate a business.

The whole topic exposes the power of information at its most dangerous.

Much of this information was being sought and held by public and private bodies long before computers were commonly available. The use of computers, however, has raised new concerns for two reasons. First, computers can sort data far more quickly than was ever possible in a manual system. The ability to process and retrieve the raw data is the real basis of the information holder's power over those who are the subjects of the information. Secondly, because data can be exchanged electronically between computers without significant human intervention, it can also easily be exchanged between databases and thus between agencies. It is, for example, perfectly possible, in a technical sense, to compare data relating to income tax, social security payments and property values for a single individual by combining data from files held by different central and local government departments. To restrict the almost unlimited potential of information holders, the state has intervened to regulate the ways in which data can be collected, stored, exchanged and used even by its own constituent parts.

This has become a very complex area of state intervention in the information field. Most industrialized countries developed data protection legislation of some kind during the 1970s and 1980s; in Britain, it was embodied in the Data Protection Act of 1984, but this was a comparative latecomer to the field. Some of the German *land* governments have had such legislation since the early 1970s, and throughout that decade the issue was a matter of growing concern in the Council of Europe, the Organization for Economic Cooperation and Development, the Commission of the European Community and UNESCO. Gradually, some generally accepted principles have developed, on the basis of which national legislation and international agreements have brought some order to a potentially chaotic field. The guiding principle of data protection in the democracies is that information should only be used for the purpose for which it is gathered, and that the subject of the information should have the right to be certain of its accuracy and relevance. The basic principles are embodied in laws which differ between jurisdictions; the principles themselves now seem to be fairly common.

In practice, however, the law is often less effective than it was intended to be; moreover, because of the very nature of the subject there is inevitable suspicion about its operation. In British law, all owners of databases that contain personal information about identifiable individuals are required to register with an agency (the Data Protection Registry) established for the purpose. When information is included in a registered database (unregistered databases are illegal), the subjects of the information have the right to assure themselves that the information is correct, up-to-date and complete. There is, however, a large number of exceptions to the general rule, most of which are designed to protect the state rather than the individual. Quite apart from the inevitable, and inevitably vague, provision that data which is considered vital to national security is exempt, there are also exemptions for data collected for the detection and prosecution of alleged criminals, and the assessment of taxes.

The real purpose of data protection law is or should be, not the protection of the state, but the protection of the individual. Registered holders of data may use it only for the purpose for which it has been collected, and may not disclose it to third parties without the permission of the data subject. The importance of this in the case of medical or financial information is obvious. On the other hand, data subjects can give permission for information to be disclosed under certain circumstances. Those whose names appear on mailing lists, for example, can give the owner of the mailing list the right to disclose it to other persons or bodies. This is normally a commercial transaction, and indeed buying and selling mailing lists has become a large-scale business in its own right. This is especially true of mail order companies and of agencies who use direct mailshots for advertising. Where the presence of a name on a mailing list (for example, of a credit card company) implies something about economic status and spending habits, the sellers of goods and services aimed at that sector of society can obviously benefit from being able to target their marketing comparatively narrowly. Moreover, it is, in practice, necessary for data subjects to ask that their names are omitted or removed from a mailing list before it is sold, rather than to ask that they shall be included. As a result, there has been a great increase in direct mail order businesses in Britain in the last decade, especially for comparatively high profit goods such as wine, or profitable services such as insurance. The computerized mailing list has all but displaced the traditional door-to-door salesman as a direct-selling mechanism to the home.

Direct sales based on computer-held mailing lists may be seen simply as a nuisance which increases the volume of junk-mail and, coincidentally, the profits of the postal services. Other uses of data are, however, more insidious. Agencies which hold data that is used to determine the creditworthiness of an individual or company are carefully regulated by law, but there have been examples of inaccurate or out-of-date information held by such an agency being used to the detriment of the data subject. It is a murky area, about which little hard evidence is available; consumer organizations, investigative journalists and consumer-oriented radio and television programmes are among those who monitor it, perhaps more effectively than the law and the state.

The issues that surround personal data held in computer databases highlight the fact that the use of computers has not been a universal and unadulterated benefit. The human ingenuity that produced computers in the first place can be applied to their misuse as well as their use. Personal data has come to have a high commercial value. Information, whether or not it is legitimately obtained or legally stored, is important for individuals and for businesses. The law has tried to afford some protection against abuse, but protection is often difficult to enforce. The potential financial rewards are substantial, and, as a result, data abuse and even theft has become one of the seamier sides of the information society.

THE ROLE OF THE STATE: FREEDOM OF INFORMATION

Data protection law generally embodies, as it does in the UK, provisions giving data subjects the right of access to information about them. There is also, however, a much broader issue concerning access to information and the 'right' of the citizen to be informed by the state. The role of the state in the circulation and storage of information is not confined to regulation. A modern state itself generates information on a massive scale, some of it for its own purposes and some for public consumption. It seeks to conceal information whose publication is perceived to be to its disadvantage, while disseminating that which is regarded as beneficial to its interests. Governments have, as we have suggested, always held huge amounts of information. The advent of computers has greatly increased the store of such information, and also, in principle, made access to it easier. The practice, however, is somewhat different.

Governments collect information through a multitude of channels. At the most basic level, almost all countries conduct a population census at regular intervals, typically decennially. The census is designed primarily to enumerate the population, but with modern data-processing methods it can also collect a great deal of other data, which can be stored, sorted and analysed for a wide variety of purposes. This might include information on such matters as occupation, educational attainments, housing conditions, religious affiliations, ethnic origins, and so on. In the UK, as in other democracies, information collected for census purposes is not published in a form which allows it to be attributed to individuals, and the documents on which the returns are made are treated as confidential for a long time (in Britain, 100 years) after the date of the census itself. After analysis, however, the anonymized data is published, and can be used for matters as diverse as academic research in sociology or the planning of transport systems.

The census provides the basic statistical data for the state, but yet more information is needed for it to function efficiently. In all democracies, there is a process of voter registration, which identifies and lists those with the right to vote in particular elections. Typically, this is a section of the population defined by age, citizenship and residence. Voter registration takes place at more frequent intervals than a full census. In the UK, it is an annual process; in some other countries, it immediately precedes an election or is part of the electoral process itself. In any case, the resulting lists are normally published and available for verification by those whose names appear on them or are wrongly omitted from them. In contrast to the census data, voter registration data is, by definition, in the public domain, and can therefore be legitimately used for many purposes. Its most obvious use is by the political parties for their own purposes such as campaigning, but it can also be exploited by commercial organizations, mail-order companies, advertisers and the like.

Both the census and the electoral register contain information collected comprehensively for public use, of which the results and some of the details will, eventually, be in the public domain. The state, however, also collects or accumulates a vast amount of data on individuals, which becomes a matter of record but is nevertheless treated as being wholly or partly confidential. Information relating to personal and corporate incomes, gathered for taxation purposes, is the most obvious example of private information which the state requires of the citizen. In the UK (although not in all countries, most notably not in the USA), income tax data is treated as being confidential between the taxation authority itself, and the individual to whom the information relates. Any dissemination of the information is at the request of the individual (to an accountant, for example), except in extreme circumstances, such as when a court investigates alleged offences in relation to the payment (or non-payment) of tax.

Company taxation information is treated differently. British companies are required by law to register their existence on a register kept at Companies House; this register, which contains basic data about the company, including its ownership and management, is open to inspection. Similar arrangements prevail in most other industrialized countries. In the case of public limited companies in the UK, they must also publish to their shareholders annual statements of their financial affairs. In that sense, the accounts (and hence, for example, the tax liabilities) of public companies are a matter of public record. Companies, however, have the same rights as individuals to privacy about much of their financial business, such as the operation of their bank accounts.

The precise nature of the information collected from or about individuals for tax purposes varies according to the nature of the direct taxation process. The taxation of income is the norm in almost all countries, with the employer usually involved in the process by deducting the tax due from an employee's salary before it is paid. The employer, however, knows nothing of any income which an employee may derive from other sources such as investments. Other forms of direct taxation also require the collection and storage of information. Property taxes are common in most countries. This necessitates the maintenance of a register both of property and of property ownership or occupation. Confidentiality rules vary from country to country. Other forms of revenue generation by the state, whether for general or specific purposes, are also dependent on the availability of accurate information. Social security contributions are usually income-related, as in the UK; these too are often deducted from earned income at source. Moreover, in almost all countries the social security system identifies individuals by a unique number, which they carry throughout their lives. In Britain and the USA, these registers compiled for social security purposes are the nearest approach to a national system of registration and identification of citizens.

In neither country is there any formal system of identity (ID) cards, although this is common in almost all other democracies and in virtually every state which is not democratic. Everyone is required to carry an identity card at all times, and to show to it to authorized officials on request. An extension of the principle of the ID card is the passport, which identifies its holder for the purposes of international travel. The information collected by registration and passport issuing agencies represents another vast data set held by the state which records information about its citizens. This by no means exhausts the list of such data. Records of driving licences and vehicle registration and taxation are increasingly comprehensive. Britain's unique system of funding its public broadcasting system creates another almost universal listing of householders in the records of the issue of television licences. All of this provides the state with a comprehensive and potentially very valuable record of the existence, location, financial affairs and activities of its citizens.

Information about individuals is collected by the state for its own administrative purposes, and in democracies its use carefully regulated by law. In general, the overarching principles of data protection apply: there is a right of verification, and information can only be used for the purposes for which it is obtained unless with the prior permission of the data subject. In practice, restraints on the state tend to be less strict than those on the private owners of databases. Moreover, abuses of the system do inevitably occur. Almost all of the data collected by the state is stored in electronic databases, and no computer system is wholly immune from unauthorized access. In addition, concern is expressed from time to time that data collected for legitimate purposes is collated for reasons of security or surveillance of individuals or organizations thought to present a threat to the state. This is a problematic area, both in law and in practice, about which there is, inevitably, much speculation but little hard information. Certainly, even democratic states can be presumed to hold some data about individual citizens which has not been collected with their participation or consent. In Britain, criminal records and other non-criminal information is kept on the Police National Computer; for reasons thought to be obvious, this is not open to public scrutiny and its records cannot therefore be validated by the data subjects. This inevitably arouses suspicion among those concerned with civil liberties and human rights.

Governments, however, do not confine their data collection activities to individuals. For purposes of registration, taxation and regulation they also collect a great deal of information about businesses, both individually and collectively. Much of this is of great political and economic significance, providing, as it does, the statistical basis for an analysis of the functioning of the economy. Both national governments, and supranational agencies like the European Union, publish huge economic data sets at regular intervals; these inform economic planning at every level down to that of the small business. Indeed, the provision of information to businesses, especially in the critical early stages of their development, is regarded as an important function of government and its information agencies.

Social and economic information collected and processed by the state or by international agencies is essentially a planning tool. It shows the role of the state as a benevolent participant in the process of information gathering and dissemination, and fulfilling its function of assisting individuals and organizations to realize their full economic potential, and hence benefit the state as a whole. There are, however, some very real problems inherent in the vast amount of data that is generated. Even librarians can become entangled in the jungle thickets of official documents, especially those from international bodies, and for individuals these thickets are all but impenetrable. Increasingly, therefore, governments and international bodies have established information agencies through which the information that they generate and publish can be made accessible to its potential beneficiaries.

The European Union has been active in this respect, with its European Documentation Centres and European Information Centres, often based on existing public sector library services. The pattern was established 50 years ago by some of the United Nations agencies, especially UNESCO with its National Commissions intended to make its work and its publications better known in member states. At national level in Britain little has been done to make government information easier to use, although the development of a comprehensive government Web site is a major advance, and, at a regional level, many local authorities have established 'information shops' and similar agencies, as well as Websites, often bypassing their own library service, through which businesses and individuals can gain access to, and take advantage of, the information which has been published and which it is their right to use. The state, in various manifestations, thus becomes an active provider as well as collector of information, for the general good.

The information collected and held by the state about its citizens and their activities, both social and economic, is one of the most potent manifestations of the information society. The state itself has become a generator, user and provider of information, and at the same time has become dependent upon it. In democracies, the use of this power is regulated by laws, some of which we have briefly explored in this chapter. Information relating to the private affairs of individuals is protected whether it is held publicly or privately with the consent of the data subject. Some publicly held information, such as the electoral register, is necessarily in the public domain, but that is explicit in the law under which it is collected and processed. In general, however, there is probably more concern about the misuse or abuse of information by the state than there is about lack of privacy. There are two approaches to this, the third area of state and legal involvement in information, which differ radically, and are perhaps best exemplified by the differences in attitude shown in the laws of the UK and the USA.

British law has always been based on the assumption that all information gathered or generated by the state is secret, and need only be revealed if this is a legal requirement. In general, the burden of proof in disputed cases rests with those seeking the information, who have to show that they need it for some proper purpose. All documents generated by government and its agencies are closed for 30 years, after which time those deposited in the Public Record Office for archival preservation are made available. There are, however, exceptions even to this rule. Some documents are protected for a hundred years or even in perpetuity. Civil servants and others who reveal information from government documents within the 30-year embargo period may be guilty of a criminal offence, as may those, principally journalists or publishers, who publish or disseminate any document or information which is revealed. In other words, British law, primarily concerned with protecting the security of the state, is based upon a presumption of secrecy. This is embodied by the principal piece of legislation upon which the law in this field depends: the Official Secrets Act.

The current (1989) version of the Official Secrets Act was intended both to simplify and to clarify the ambiguities in its predecessors of 1911 and 1920. It remains the case, however, that it fundamentally inhibits the communication, publication or dissemination of information generated or collected by the state and its agencies. Few would question that some of this information is legitimately restricted in the interests of national security; this might include, for example, information relating to defence establishments and weapons systems, or information assembled about the covert agents of foreign states operating in the UK. The problem is that the Act, like all secret systems, is open not only to abuse but also to the suspicion of abuse. The Act does allow a defence of 'public interest', under which a person accused of an offence can argue that the disclosure of information was for the general good. This defence has been successfully used by civil servants and others, but the Act remains unpopular in many quarters. Further reform is on the political agenda, but the whole subject has been a matter of fundamental disagreement between those of differing political opinions, and is so contentious that reform may take a very long time.

Even in Britain, there are exceptions to blanket secrecy about the activities of government. The proceedings of Parliament and of local councils are, with a few exceptions, conducted in public, and both the proceedings themselves, and the background papers which facilitate the business, are in the public domain. At local government level, the minutes and papers of committee meetings, through which the detailed business of councils is actually conducted, are also public, but, at national level, what might be thought to be comparable documents, such as the minutes of the Cabinet and its committees, are protected under the 30-year rule. In general, however, the law, especially, the Local Government (Access to Information) Act of 1985, carefully regulates what must be made available, while continuing to assume that everything else is secret.

A very different attitude prevails in the USA. The Freedom of Information Act of 1975 effectively put all federal government information and documents into the public domain, unless the government could prove that national security was endangered by publication. This approach is diametrically opposite to that in the UK, although not an unmixed blessing. When the Act was first passed, some journalists in Washington complained that the Government was providing so much information that they were unable to cope with it and that they had been able to work more efficiently when they had to ferret out for themselves what they needed to know! Nevertheless, the distinction between the two approaches exemplifies two differing views of the relationship between the state and its own citizens. Freedom of information legislation has been proposed in Britain from time to time, but has so far developed only in a very lacklustre fashion. The present British government is, however, committed to it, and legisation is planned for the next year or so.

Intellectual property, data protection and freedom of information all exemplify different aspects of the three-way relationship between information itself, the state and the individual citizen. In each of these cases, the role of the state has been to intervene in the chain of communication between the source and the user of information. Almost inevitably such intervention is inhibitory. The stimulatory role of intellectual property law, in encouraging the publishers of books, the owners of databases and others to continue to develop such products, is a coincidental benefit and a *post facto* justification of a law designed essentially to protect the interests of authors and publishers in their capacity as the owners of property. Data protection legislation, although designed to protect individuals from unwarranted intrusion on their privacy, can, in practice, be used for commercial purposes which do involve some such intrusion, how ever trivial it may be thought to be. Freedom of information is the least widely understood and the least developed area of the three. This is significant, for freedom of information can only be beneficial to citizens if it is considered that a well-informed citizen derives benefits from the information that is acquired. The state, and those who constitute its government and bureaucracy, is exposed whenever there is open access to information.

THE ROLE OF THE STATE: CENSORSHIP

The fourth and final major area of state intervention in the communication chain is the oldest of all: censorship. The concept is a familiar one, and has been so for centuries. The state seeks to prevent the publication or dissemination of information and opinion which it considers to be detrimental to its own understanding of its interests. The nature of the perceived detriment may vary. In early modern Europe, for example, Catholic and Protestant authorities censored each other's religious writings on grounds which were both moral and political. In some Islamic countries it is illegal to sell or distribute the Bible, as it was in some of the former socialist countries in eastern Europe. Overt political censorship has significantly diminished since 1989, but in many developing countries opposition newspapers have great difficulty in surviving, partly because governments can and do prevent their circulation, but, more insidiously, because pro-government newspapers are heavily subsidized, receive favourable treatment from government and are more widely available at more affordable prices.

Censorship of the printed word has, however, become significantly more difficult as a result of modern technological developments. During the 1991 attempted *coup d'état* in what was then still the Soviet Union, the anti-coup forces kept their allies in other parts of the country informed by using fax connections which had not, in an act of incredible folly and oversight, been cut. Indeed, for much of the last 20 years of its existence, the Soviet state was severely undermined by one technology after another. Photocopying, and even duplicating machines, made possible the production of underground literature on a small but significant scale, with far less risk of detection than would have been incurred by using conventional printing equipment, even if that had been available. Short-wave radio broadcasts, some overtly propagandist (such as Voice of America or Radio Free Europe) and one or two merely objective (most notably the BBC World Service), overcame some of the ignorance created by media wholly owned and controlled by the state. Towards the very end, the growing ease of international telecommunications, fax and e-mail ate yet further into the decaying fabric of the Soviet state. In the last months of European Communism, the availability of news through satellite television created a 'copycat' movement which destabilized one regime after another from Germany to Siberia. State Communism in eastern Europe was not destroyed by information technology, but it is clear from the experience of those countries that the new technologies of information and communication made it difficult and finally impossible for governments to continue to exercise untrammelled control over the dissemination of information in comparatively advanced societies.

Not for the first time, however, we confront a technological paradox; the very developments that have made censorship more difficult have also made it easier. As we have seen, most information about current affairs comes from television and radio, not from newspapers. Those media are comparatively easy for the state to control. In some countries, the state is indeed the monopoly owner of broadcasting systems, but even where a more or less free market prevails, there are still some controls. The most important is economic, for the capital costs of television production and broadcasting are astronomically high. Competition is possible, and has been achieved in most industrialized countries, but it is only between very large companies, and it is comparatively limited in scope. Even in the USA, which probably has the least regulated television industry in the world, licences to broadcast are granted on a regional basis, and some restrictions are placed on the extent of competition permitted between companies. At the same time, however, technology has made the regulation of broadcasting more difficult. Satellite television is, by its very nature international, and there is evidence that the news services, especially CNN, have actually influenced the development of events in some countries by making information available to their citizens which national broadcasters were forced to suppress.

The high capital costs of entering the information market-place are only one way in which technology can help a censor. Telecommunications links are as vital to links between computers as they are to conventional telephone connections. These too are normally the subject of complex regulatory regimes, in which the state plays a major role either as regulator or as active participant. Just as the information poor are excluded from many of the benefits of the information technology revolution, so some of the information rich may have their benefits restricted by the control which the state can exercise over their access to communications systems.

There is, however, a great difference between regulation of communications systems, which could be argued to be the only way to maintain a comprehensive and orderly service, and overt interference with the information and opinion which is disseminated through those systems. In many western countries, most notably the USA, the freedom of the press is the subject of legal or constitutional guarantees. Like freedom of information, however, freedom of the press is a fine phrase and an attractive idea, but it has sometimes proved rather less easy to implement as a practical policy.

Total freedom to publish and disseminate without control of any kind has never been institutionalized, although it may occasionally have happened in revolutionary situations from England in 1642 to Russia in 1991. The freedom of the press is limited both economically and legally. The legal restrictions vary immensely, but even at their lightest, they include some limitations on the publication of defamatory statements about individuals, and usually on the publication of material deemed to be morally objectionable. Both of these areas are even more difficult to define than overt political censorship, but both represent serious inhibitions on the free communication of information. The understanding of defamation varies in different legal systems. In the USA, for example, a true statement cannot normally be libellous, whereas in Britain it can; the British criterion is whether the subject's reputation is damaged rather than whether the information is accurate. Indeed, libel is an area in which participants in public life in Britain are exceptionally litigious, often making use of such devices as an injunction under which a court can forbid the publication of information until there is time to hold a full trial which will determine whether or not it is defamatory or otherwise illegal. The laws of libel are a formidable obstacle to a free press, and are open to abuse by the unscrupulous. The late James Goldsmith was a master of the art of using the law in this way to protect his reputation and to attack his enemies during his lifetime; even in Britain, however, the libel laws do not protect the dead.

Moral censorship rests on even less certain foundations. Both secular states such as the USA and France, as well as secularized societies like the UK, still retain legislation which attempts to prescribe the acceptable moral limits of publication in many formats. The pre-distribution censorship of films and videos is commonplace even in the democracies. In practice, many film producers, like the television production companies, exercise a form of self-censorship in order to keep within the boundaries of the law and what is socially acceptable. Moral censorship of printed matter is even more difficult, although pre-publication censorship, equivalent to the pre-release classification of movies and videos, is not normally practised in democratic states. In Britain, the 1959 Obscene Publications Act turned juries into literary critics by requiring them to determine whether or not a work had 'literary merit', for, if it had, it was less likely to fall within the scope of the law. Like similar legislation elsewhere, the Act has brought the law into disrepute and ridicule, without seriously inhibiting the illicit publication of the pornography at which it was, presumably, aimed.

The Internet has opened up a whole new field of debate about moral censorship. There are Websites which are the electronic equivalent of pornographic magazines, and these have perhaps emphasized the difficulty of defining what is acceptable. Images which can be openly sold in newsagents' shops (however distasteful) can hardly be prevented from appearing on the Web. But the Internet also provides a channel for clearly illegal material (child pornography being the most obvious example), and there must also be a question about the use of publicly supported networks (such as JANET) to access such material for non-academic purposes. In practice, blanket regulation is all but impossible without a politically unacceptable level of intervention in the operation of the Internet, but codes of conduct have been developed by service providers with sanctions (such as denial of access) against 'offenders'.

Moral censorship, like the other matters discussed in this chapter, represents an aspect of the state's role in the communication of information. It is inevitable that the state should have such a role. It is in the very nature of the information society that vast quantities of information are stored and are theoretically available. The state, at the very least, has a duty to its citizens to protect them against the abuse of that stored information. At the same time, the state, on behalf of its citizens, has an interest in ensuring that the channels of information and communications can operate effectively. The difficulty is the cost of maintaining them. The infrastructure of information supply, through whatever medium, is now so expensive that without some form of protection it is doubtful whether it could exist at all. This consideration is the ultimate justification for intellectual property laws, especially in relation to copyright, and for state intervention in the regulation of telecommunications and broadcasting.

CONTEMPORARY DILEMMAS: THE ISSUES REDEFINED

If we take this comparatively benevolent view of the role of the state, we can see both data protection and freedom of information legislation, where they exist, as being further manifestations of the liberal state protecting its citizens. Both are designed to ensure that citizens are well informed about those matters which they have a right to know, while simultaneously protecting their personal privacy. The problem, which has been implicit throughout this chapter, is in defining the limits of the public and the private domain; it is an issue which arises frequently in the so called 'public interest' defence against charges of breaches of official secrecy and state security. If the state is merely the corporate embodiment of its citizens, and exists solely to represent their interests and their collective will, then it could be argued that the right to know is absolute, and that the state, as in the American system, must be able to justify depriving citizens of any information of which it itself is possessed. In practice, the rights of individuals are generally far more limited than this position implies.

These issues have always been important in the democracies, for they concern the very nature of the democratic process itself. It could be argued that information lies at the heart of the process, for it is only an informed citizen who can cast an informed vote. On the other hand, the state also has a protective role in relation to its citizens. There is general agreement that this includes protecting the state itself against its external enemies, and that this must certainly influence its policies towards the provision and concealment of information. There is less agreement about the extent to which the state, embodied in an elected government, has the right to protect itself against its own citizens by depriving them of information which might make them critical of it, or which, in its judgment, might be morally deleterious to it or to them.

Many of these long-standing issues have been exacerbated and re-emphasized by the information and communications revolution of the late twentieth century. The proponents of stricter moral censorship of television, videos and the Internet, for example, insist that their easy availability in virtually every home imposes a duty on producers, broadcasting organizations and other information providers to maintain high standards. There is, of course, no common agreement on what these standards should be, nor on a politically and socially acceptable mechanism for enforcing them. Even this debate, however, familiar as it still is, could be argued to be losing its relevance. Satellite broadcasting is extra-territorial; we are years and possibly decades away from international treaties which will impose uniform moral regimes on transnational and international broadcasters. Domestic use of simple technologies (like video recorders or satellite television decoders) is almost impossible to control. Film censorship, for example, was viable for so long as movies could only be watched on television or at the cinema; the advent of video has made it impossible to enforce except against the shops from which the videos are bought or rented. Once they have been obtained, nothing can prevent their private viewing, any more than it is possible to prevent the use of printed pornography once it has evaded any laws which attempt to prevent its distribution. Using the law against networked pornography is also proving to be very difficult, although not impossible. Technology has not won the battle against the censors, but it has redrawn the map of the battlefield and rewritten the rules of engagement.

The balance may, in due course, change again; whether it does or not, technology has fundamentally changed the role of the state in the information transfer process. Historically, the state has been a spectator, a protector and a regulator. Intermittently, it has also been a participant, as propagandist or monopoly supplier. Now it is, increasingly, a competitor in the information market-place where it is only one of many powerful agencies, which seeks to manipulate the market and customers, as well as being a collector of information and subject to its own rules about the storage, use and dissemination of the information which it collects. The balance between the obligation of the state to provide information and its duty to protect itself by secrecy has been struck in different ways in different countries. In all states, however, even in the most open democracies, there is clearly a distinction, however its boundaries are defined, between the public and private spheres of government information. Similarly, there is a distinction, equally difficult to define, between the state as a provider of factual information and the state as the generator of propaganda.

Promoting its own country is a necessary part of the function of any government. Many countries have developed institutions and agencies which have a specific responsibility to do so. Some of these agencies are overtly propagandist, while others concentrate on the promotion of educational and cultural links with other countries. In either case, it can be cogently argued that national self-promotion is one of the legitimate functions of government. Domestically, however, this can easily slide into political propaganda whose purpose is partisan rather than general. In totalitarian states, the sole purpose of government information agencies is to disseminate the information (whether true or not) which portrays the government in the best light. Suppression of unwelcome truths, favourable interpretations of events and the invention or falsification of 'facts' are all part of the armoury of the propagandist. Propaganda, in various guises, has been a tool of the state since states first existed, but the evolution and development of sophisticated systems of communication have greatly facilitated its use and increased its effectiveness.

Almost as soon as it was invented, the printing press was adopted for propagandist purposes. It has indeed been forcefully argued that printing was a major factor in the success of the Protestant Reformation. The proposition is, by its nature, neither provable nor refutable, but it is unquestionable that the easy availability of a simple technology for communicating information and opinion over time and distance was a significant difference between the sixteenth century and earlier periods in which reform of the Church had been attempted. Newspapers were first used as propaganda tools during the Thirty Years War in Germany (1618–48) and the contemporary Civil War in England

(1642–9); they have been used in every European war since then, and throughout the world as European technology and influence spread across the globe.

It has, however, been the twentieth century which has seen the triumph of propaganda. Totalitarian states of both the left and the right, and both governments and oppositions in the democracies, exploited the potential of the new mass media. The first medium to be used in this way was the cinema, seen by Lenin as the most important means of bringing 'information' to the people of the newly created Soviet Union. In Germany after 1933, the Nazis exploited films in the same way, both by overt propaganda, as in the newsreels, and by more subtle means. Two of the greatest film-makers of the 1920s and 1930s, Eisenstein in the USSR and Rehfenstahl in Germany, for all their undoubted artistic achievements, were propagandists working for the success of political programmes in which they profoundly believed.

Radio also served a propagandist purpose. Hitler, a brilliant orator, exploited it to the full. So did two of his bitterest foes, Churchill and Roosevelt. All were masters of the spoken word. Roosevelt, in particular, developed a radio style, very different from traditional platform oratory, which brought something like domesticity to his promotion of his administration's policies into almost every American home. These examples show how difficult it is to define the concept of propaganda. The term is perhaps too emotive, too suggestive of falsehood and the promotion of the undesirable. What is certain, however, is that the mass media of the early and middle decades of the twentieth century gave politicians unprecedented access to those over whom they ruled, and upon whose support and votes some of them depended.

The use of the media by political parties and governments continues to be a political issue in its own right. At the same time, however, there is what is probably generally regarded as a legitimate area of government activity in information provision. Although sometimes the subject of political controversy, it is broadly accepted that such comparatively neutral matters as anonymized or statistical information relating to health, social security benefits, personal safety, crime prevention and the like are proper subjects for information dissemination by governments. Like other information providers, governments will use whatever seems to be the most efficient and cost-effective means of reaching its target audience. This might be advertisements in newspapers or in the cinema or on television, or leaflets provided through libraries, Citizens' Advice Bureaux or even directly to every household. Like advertisers, government agencies have to undertake appropriate market research to determine how they can best get their message to the intended recipients.

This reveals yet again the conflict which is inherent in government involvement in information collection and dissemination. On the one hand, its concern is with secrecy, and on the other, with dissemination. It has both constraints and requirements imposed on it by the law. The unique ability of government to collect information at a national level, and to make it available both nationally and internationally, makes it an important operator in the information market-place. Governments are major publishers both of priced and free publications. They are, either directly or indirectly, the principal funders of public, school and university libraries. At the same time, they are the protectors of vast quantities of personal data, and also of information which they regard as being potentially too damaging to the national interest to be made available at all. The intrinsic contradictions in these many and varied roles are obvious, and the potential for conflicts of interest between one part of government and another, and, even more importantly, between governors and governed, are equally clear.

Even governments, however, must make use of channels of communication provided by the private sector, and take account of their influence. The relationship between government and the media in an open society can never be a comfortable one; indeed, it might be argued that it should not be. On the other hand, governments have a regulatory role in ensuring that the media, and the providers of telecommunications systems, work in a way which, while not inhibiting profit, is for the general good. Questions which can be formulated about the role of the state in controlling the flow of information in a free society inevitably lead into even more difficult questions about the role of the media and the providers of telecommunications networks in such a society, some of which go beyond our present concerns.

It is one of the hallmarks of democracy that the press and the broadcasting media are not under the editorial control of government, although the extent of their freedom varies greatly from one country to another. In the USA, for example, there is almost total freedom within broad constitutional and legal constraints relating to libel, security, and the like. In some west European countries, on the other hand, at least until recently, the government exercised substantial control over the output of the state broadcasting organizations in both radio and television; this was the case in both France and Italy. Recent technological developments have fundamentally changed the ability of the state to intervene in the affairs of broadcasters. The internationalization of television through the use of satellite transmission has effectively undermined the power of the state to control what is received, even when reception is theoretically illegal. In practice, power over the content of satellite television rests almost entirely with the owners and employees of the broadcasting organizations. Satellite news services, such as those of CNN and the BBC's World Service Television, have revolutionized the availability of news and comment in many countries whose own broadcasters are under strict state control. In that sense, satellite television has broken the state monopoly.

Conversely, power has been transferred to the media corporations themselves. Even more than governments, these organizations can control and manipulate the flow of information. Where cross-media ownership is permitted, so that the same company can be involved in, for example, television and newspapers, this makes the media giants far more powerful than any democratic state has ever aspired to be, and far more powerful in practice than all but the most successful of totalitarian states have succeeded in being. Both the press and television exercise great influence by their selection of news and by their presentation of it. Even where 'objectivity' is sought, the very process of selection (which is inevitable) means that it cannot truly be achieved. The role of the journalist, the editor and the media owner thus becomes that of a gatekeeper of information and former of opinion.

The intervention of a democratic state in this process is minimal, but that is not necessarily beneficial to the individual citizen seeking reliable information. There are indeed some developments which go some way towards counterbalancing the potential influence of the transnational mass media, but they are limited in scale and scope. Desktop publishing systems, for example, have made it possible for very small organizations with limited capital to issue their own newsletters and information sheets. Distribution, however, remains a problem, and can usually only be achieved on a very local level, or through the use of mailing lists which are costly to assemble, maintain and service. Public access television, based in local communities, is not unknown where cable networks exist, and will become more common, but cannot hope to countervail the influence of the network broadcast services and the transnational satellite channels. The World Wide Web has the greatest potential of all, for it gives every user the power to publish.

It is probably in the field of computer networks that new technology offers the greatest potential for bypassing existing commercial and governmental information and communications systems. As we saw in Chapter 4, the academic networks which have been developed throughout the industrialized world are now linked through the Internet to permit virtually uncontrolled, and normally uncharged, access to vast stores of information. The present anarchy of the Internet, which reflects its unplanned origin and growth, allows anyone with network access to search for information of interest, and to contribute to thousands of ongoing debates, use public access databases, and the like. The networks allow individual information-seekers to search directly and personally for their information, and for individual providers to make such information available with virtually no editorial, commercial or political control.

It is doubtful whether this freedom will continue to prevail. Abuse of the system and perhaps fear of its potential will inevitably lead to regulation. The development of the information superhighways will necessarily bring in its wake a regulatory regime comparable to that for telecommunications networks. It may be stringent or light, but it will, however mildly, impose a degree of control. The complex relationship between information, the state and citizen will thus continue to evolve. As it does so, the role of the intermediary will also change, for the ever-growing size and complexity of information sources and systems inevitably means that information-seekers will need help. Some of this comes from within the systems themselves, but there is still a need for gatekeepers and guides who can assist individuals to exploit to the full the vast stores of information which are available to them. It is the role of these functionaries – the information professionals – that we shall consider in Chapter 7.

7

THE INFORMATION PROFESSION

The information needs of governments, institutions, businesses and individuals can only be satisfied if they can be matched to the available resources, and those resources then be made accessible to the potential users. The quantity and complexity of information, and of the systems and services through which it can be provided, have grown in tandem with the growth of our information needs and our dependence upon effective provision. The information professionals would seem to be the intermediaries between information sources, information systems and information users. They might be – perhaps should be – key players in the information society. In this chapter, we shall explore their role.

THE INFORMATION PROFESSION: A DOMAIN DELINEATED

If we consider the various issues which have been discussed in the previous chapters of this book, we can identify three strands of information which interlock but which are essentially different. These might be defined as:

- public information;
- personal information;
- private information.

We shall also need to consider three similarly interwoven aspects of information storage and provision. These are:

- information sources
- information networks and systems
- information agencies.

The distinction between them is critical to understanding the proper role of the information professional.

For our purposes, *public* information is information which is intended to be in the public domain. This statement, however, needs some further refinement. The phrase 'public domain' is not used here as it is used by an intellectual property lawyer; in that context, it means information, texts, designs, and so on which are no longer protected by the relevant laws, and can be freely used, copied and reproduced, like a book whose copyright has expired. In the present context, the phrase is used less precisely, to mean information which is intended to be publicly available within the normal constraints of law and commerce. The information in any book is in the public domain in this sense, even though the copyright is not. The book has been written to be circulated (by purchase and perhaps by subsequent loan) and then read in whole or in part. There are indeed some factors which might inhibit its unlimited circulation. It has to be bought either by the reader or by someone (such as a librarian) on the reader's behalf. A non-purchaser who seeks to read a book must have access to a library which stocks it, and then find it in stock when it is sought, and so on. These, however, are minor obstacles, which are of some practical importance but which do not affect the basic principle that the clear intention of the author and publisher of this or any other book is that it should be available to the public at large.

Public domain information – collected, analysed and prepared for use – takes many forms. A conventionally published printed book is perhaps a paradigm of the phenomenon, but by no means the only example. Statistical information assembled by governments, for example, is available through various publications, printed, photographic and electronic, and, in some cases, also through online systems or perhaps videotext. Some of it is free of charge; the most spectacular growth of such information is on the Internet. Some (such as online access to certain databases or some government publications) is very expensive to obtain. The principle, however, is unaffected: the information is intended for public use, and the monetary cost of obtaining it is no more than a financial transaction designed to offset the costs of providing it and perhaps to generate a profit which will sustain the business of the providers.

Once this concept of public domain information is accepted, the distinction between it and *private* information is comparatively easy to establish and define. It is simply information which is not intended for public circulation, having been assembled and stored to satisfy some private purpose. Uncontentious examples include marketing information assembled by a company, which would be valuable to its competitors (and probably acquired more cheaply by copying) and whose general availability would therefore be disadvantageous to those who had incurred the expense of collecting it. There is probably no serious disagreement about the legitimacy of the general concept of commercial confidentiality of this kind, and hence of the basic principle of the legitimate existence of information which is not publicly available. Other issues are less straightforward. Governments and their agencies are also involved in this sphere of information, and, as has been suggested in Chapter 6, there are different views of the proper boundaries between the private and public domains, symbolized in the different attitudes embodied in the Official Secrets Act in the UK and the Freedom of Information Act in the USA.

The distinction which is being suggested between private and *personal* information is essentially that between information relating to institutions, organizations, companies and groups, on the one hand, and, on the other hand, information relating to identifiable individuals. Again, however, there are few absolutes. While it would be generally agreed that information relating to a person's health, for example, is indeed private and should be confidential, there are circumstances in which it inevitably and properly becomes known to others. In the case of health information, the 'others' include doctors and paramedics who treat the data subject, and, with the data subject's consent, might also include insurance companies or employers. Professional ethical codes are sometimes as important as the law in regulating the use and dissemination of private information. To develop this example further, there may be ethical considerations about informing a patient's family, or even patients themselves, about the diagnosis or prognosis of a particular medical condition.

Moreover, some personal information might, with the data subject's passive consent, be made available to others, perhaps in a non-attributable form. Information collected for census purposes, for example, or by market research companies, is not published in a form which allows individuals to be identified, even though this identification may be known to the data collector and be stored in the data files. In some circumstances, data subjects may even allow attributable data to be made available; for example, in giving consent for one's name and address to be on a particular mailing list, one may give or refuse consent for that mailing list to be sold to other organizations.

THE ROLE OF THE INFORMATION PROFESSIONAL

We turn now to our second set of factors which underpin our understanding of the functions and responsibilities of the information professional.

Information *sources* are the essential basis upon which all information provision rests. For much of the last 500 years, this has primarily meant printed sources, although orality was never, as we saw in Chapters 1 and 2, entirely lost or forgotten. In the last hundred years, the development of new media for the storage and dissemination of information products has multiplied the variety of sources, and has been a factor in greatly increasing their number. The contents of such sources of information are more readily accessible when they are deliberate creations rather than accidental accumulations. Even if the accretion of information (or information media) is partly random, its effective use requires systematic organization. A library is a useful paradigm here. Even the most systematically assembled library can only be used if its contents are recorded in an equally systematic way, and those records provide access to the books in the library. The catalogue, and perhaps the classification of the books by subject (which may be reflected in their order on the shelves), thus becomes a key tool in the effective exploitation of the library as an information resource.

All information sources, to be effective, need to be similarly systematic in their organization. In books, for example, the table of contents, the index, and even such mundane matters as the page numbers, are all part of a design which allows the book to be used. The arrangement of the data is even more important. Even books which consist principally of continuous prose are easier to use if there is an alphabetic index to their subject matter. Some books are actually built around such an index; a dictionary is perhaps the most perfect example, but there are, of course, many other reference books which work on the same principle. In considering the sources of information, therefore, we are looking at their format and their arrangement, as well as at their contents. The same basic principles apply, as we have seen, to the design of a database to facilitate access. In the same way, a well-designed Website is easy to find and easy to navigate, with well developed and logically selected links to other pages and sites.

It is, however, the content which is the *raison d'être* of the book or other information source. If the source is to be used effectively and confidently, there have to be some standards for making a qualitative assessment of it. For all factual information, the minimal requirement is accuracy, so far as that can be attained; to validate that, it is common practice to give a source for the information, or at least some account of other sources from which it can be verified. In the past, this quality control has rested largely with editors and publishers. As we have seen in Chapters 3 and 4, however, traditional methods are breaking down even in the publishing industry, for both economic and technological reasons. On the Internet, there are only whatever standards Webmasters and other information providers apply to themselves.

Information *networks and systems* are the means by which information is stored and disseminated. Both terms are now usually associated with the use of computers, but their applications can usefully be extended to other methods of storage and dissemination. In the library world, for example, the word 'network' has long been used to describe a group of libraries which collaborate or interact with one other for some purpose such as interlending or other cooperative activities intended to benefit their clients. The basic concept of the network is that of providing a communications link, regardless of the form which that link might take. We can properly refer to a road network, or a telephone network, as well as an information network or a computer network.

Such networks are essential in the provision of information, since no individual provider or agency can be in possession of all the information which might be required by clients. It is only through networks which link providers with one other, and with the sources to which each has access, that clients can be fully and effectively served. The mechanism that facilitates this is most easily described as an information system. This might indeed be a complex computer-based system, it might be very simple local agreements about library cooperation or it might be informal personal contacts. In essence, however, they are the same; all exist to anticipate specific demand in the hope that such a demand can, through their operation, be more effectively met.

There is no absolute reason why information provision should be institutionalized, but, in practice, it is normally delivered through an *agency*. Again, the word is used with a very wide and general application. The agency may be an individual (more properly called an *agent*) or it may be an organization or institution. It may be part of a larger body, like the information section in a business, or it may be a distinctive body in its own right like a national library. Perhaps most agencies, like the libraries of universities, fall somewhere in between. The precise distinctions do not concern us. The important point is that an information agency (or agent) provides a point of contact between the information-seeker and the information which is contained in and derived from various sources and then delivered through networks and systems to the end-user.

In bringing together the concepts of public, private and personal information on the one hand, and information sources, information networks and systems, and information agencies, on the other, we can begin to define the concept of the information professional. At each stage in the various processes that have been described both in the first few pages of this chapter and in the earlier chapters of this book, we can identify some familiar occupational groups who are involved in them. These most obviously include publishers, librarians and archivists, but there are many others. The authors and compilers of information sources clearly play a critical role, and they must be added to our list. The managers of information networks and systems provide the essential infrastructure for information delivery to end-users; some such managers call themselves 'librarians' but many others do not. The title may be as vague as 'information officer' or as apparently precise as 'system manager'. Do all of these groups constitute a single profession? If they do, what are its characteristics, and what is its role in an increasingly information dependent society?

THE WORK OF THE INFORMATION PROFESSIONAL

Some of these questions can more easily be answered if we consider a few exemplary cases of those who work with information. In Chapter 3, we looked at aspects of the work of the authors and publishers of books, and at the means of book production, distribution and sale. In the simplest case of a book written by one person, that person – the author – is the originator, analyst and guarantor of the information which the book contains. Authors may seek to bolster their own authority by citing that of others; this is the purpose of citations of sources and similar devices. The substantive intellectual input of the author is in the interpretation, selection and presentation of the material, much of which may already, as a collection of related but separate facts, be familiar to many of the book's readers. The publisher's role is quite different. The publishing function is essentially that of facilitation, making possible the production and distribution of the author's work by providing both the capital investment and technical skills that are needed to enable it to reach its intended market and audience. Where are the information skills in this process?

If we see the writing, publishing and sale of books as part of a continuous chain of the communication of information from author to reader, then we can cogently argue that both author and publisher are indeed professionally involved with information. In neither case, however, is this to be understood as meaning that they necessarily possess or need specific professional qualifications or training. The publisher may indeed do so, although in British publishing this is still comparatively uncommon, but the author almost certainly will not. Both require, no doubt, a good general education and high levels of literacy and its associated skills, but these are not acquired through the sort of formal processes of examination and monitoring of practice which we associate with professions such as law or medicine. Perhaps it would be more terminologically accurate to say that authors and publishers are occupationally involved with information, although, for reasons which will be suggested later, the very word 'professional' is becoming less exclusive and defining than it used to be.

When we move away from the simple model of the single-authored book, however, we have to consider different factors. Even in a comparatively straightforward case, such as a volume of essays by several writers with an editor, the role of the editor is not only intellectually different from that of an author working alone but also involves other skills. The editor will, for example, be expected to impose a uniformity of technical style on the contributors. This is not an aesthetic matter of prose style as it might be understood by a literary critic, but style in the narrower technical sense, such as forms of bibliographical references, and the almost invisible issues of uniformity of spellings where there are alternatives (-ise/-ize endings, for example), hierarchies of headings and subheadings, and the use of typographical devices such as bold and italic. These issues, which fundamentally affect the readability and hence the utility of the book, are essentially professional. They may be undertaken by an employee or agent of the publisher, or by the editor of the volume, acting *de facto* in that capacity. Whoever is responsible, that person is making information more accessible to the user, and functioning, in part, as an information professional.

If we consider the case of the compiler and editor of a reference book or (analogously for this purpose) a database, these issues are further clarified. A reference tool, whether it is on paper or in electronic form, is only as efficient as its design. Basic decisions about the order and form of entries, and the means of accessing the information through indexes and other devices, will determine how well, and perhaps even whether, it can be used. Few reference books, and probably no public databases, are compiled by a single individual. Therefore, rules are needed which systematically regulate the entries and can be unambiguously applied by all the contributors, perhaps over many years. To the librarian, a cataloguing code is the most obvious and familiar example of such a set of rules. Without such a code, a catalogue makes no sense. When such a code is properly written and uniformly applied, however, the standardization and compatibility of catalogues is assured. During the last 20 years, the *Anglo-American Cataloguing Rules* in their second edition (AACR2), have been adopted throughout the world as a standard code. Closely related to them have been other forms of bibliographical standardization like the MARC format for machine-readable catalogues, and the International Standard Book Description (ISBD). As a result, it has been possible to create compatible catalogues in different institutions. Libraries have been able to share the costs of cataloguing and to 'buy' their catalogue records from a central source such as a national bibliographical agency or a book supplier. Costs have been cut, standards raised and access simplified. All of this has been achieved through imposing uniform standards on electronic databases.

On a smaller scale, the same principle applies to any multi-authored work of reference. A dictionary or encyclopedia has an internal logic and arrangement to which all contributors are expected to adhere, and which the editors will impose on the contributions of those who deviate from it. In a dictionary, for example, editorial policy will determine whether each word is defined, whether an etymology is given, whether there are examples of usage, and so on. The same principle applies to all reference works of this kind. It also applies, and perhaps even more strictly, to a database. The obvious advantages of an electronic database over a printed source – currency and ease of access – can be achieved only if the database design is appropriate. This means that before a single entry is compiled and entered, the designer must try to anticipate both the needs and the expertise of the user. There must also be quality control mechanisms to ensure that each entry complies exactly with the rules which have been determined. When such systems have been devised and implemented, however, there is no limit to the number of contributors who can augment the database, nor, given appropriate network access, any limitation on their locations.

When we consider the compilation of bibliographies, catalogues and reference books, and indeed the design of public access databases, we can perhaps no longer so clearly define the boundaries of professional information work. The editors and the publishers are engaged in a joint enterprise to which each bring their own expertise, but these areas of expertise necessarily overlap. The closeness with which they must work together, often over a long period of time, is quite different from the classical model of the author–publisher relationship.

These examples suggest that the concept of the 'publisher' as an information professional needs to be extended beyond the traditional understanding of the publisher's role. Indeed, the boundaries between publishing and the other functions of information compilation, production and distribution, are, as we have seen in Chapter 3, already blurring and perhaps dissolving. When an author 'writes' a book onto a disk, and the file which is created eventually drives the phototypesetter which produces the printing plate, the traditional functions of author, publisher's editor, copy editor and compositor have all changed; that of the compositor may even have been eliminated. The disaggregation and recombination of skills in this model is typical of the changes being wrought by the use of computers in the information world; traditional boundaries are being eroded and there is convergence between traditionally separate activities.

LIBRARIANS AND LIBRARIES: ARCHETYPES IN TRANSITION

In considering some aspects of the work of the librarian, this process is perhaps even more obvious. In some ways, librarians are the archetypal information professionals. Indeed, the terms are often used synonymously, with perhaps a suggestion that the 'information professional' is more modern and forward-looking than the traditional (an epithet increasingly attached) 'librarian'. No such synonymy is being suggested here, but 'librarianship', as it is normally understood and practised, is certainly intended to be encompassed by the broader concept. Historically, the librarian has been the collector and curator of books, making arrangements for them to be inventoried, stored and used, by means of such devices and mechanisms as catalogues, classification schemes, circulation systems, and the like. Inevitably, this has also made librarians the managers of the institutions in which these activities take place, and therefore managers of financial, human and physical resources.

In the last 20–30 years, however, the role of the librarian has been subject to great change. To some extent this has been a change of emphasis. There is an explicit recognition that it is the provision of books and information to users which is the driving force of the librarian's work, and that for most users the source of either is a matter of indifference. Quality of service is measured by speed and accuracy of fulfilment of users' demands, not by the number of books in stock or even cruder statistical data such as the number of loans. Even so, the custodial role has not been forgotten, and has not become irrelevant. Information sources have a physical existence, even if it is on a disk in a computer at a site many thousands of miles away from the point of consultation. The information can be accessed only if the medium is sufficiently stable for it to survive. Nevertheless, the custodianship implied by the preservation of such a source is a means to an end, rather than an end itself.

The change of attitude, embodied in the explicit recognition of the primacy of the user rather than the source, was under way long before information technology made its major impact on librarianship from the mid-1970s onwards. Since that time, change has been rapid and profound. The most fundamental tool of the librarian – the catalogue – has been transformed beyond recognition. The online public access catalogue (OPAC) – in effect a bibliographic database of the library's holdings – offers a vast range of services which were never previously available to users. Freed from the physical restraints of the traditional card catalogue, which at its best (rarely attained) normally offered access only by author, subject and title, the user can now search for holdings in a way which meets individual needs rather than the convenience of the managers of the catalogue. This, however, is only the beginning.

Other computer-based tools have wrought a similar revolution in access to information itself. Databases, whether accessed online on distant hosts or locally or through a network on CD-ROM, are supplanting, as has already been suggested, many reference sources which have formerly been available only in print. This fact alone has changed both the technicalities and economics of information provision. Effective use of a database requires some training; it is difficult to use it without some instruction, and almost impossible to use it well. The instruction may be no more than a printed sheet accompanying a CD-ROM – the equivalent of the preface to a reference book – but such instruction (unlike the use of the preface) is essential rather than desirable. Technology gives access to vast quantities of information, and yet has made access somewhat more difficult.

Far from eliminating the librarian, the use of technology as the basis of information service provision has highlighted the need for people with special skills who can help information seekers. Nevertheless, the role of those people has changed. In academic libraries, in particular, librarians are increasingly working as the trainers and guides of a computer-literate generation of students who need to be taught the specifics of information searching and retrieval in their own disciplines. In effect, librarians are passing on to their users some of what were traditionally regarded as their own unique professional skills. Despite the inevitable and desirable survival of some mediated searches, in which librarians work on behalf of users, librarians increasingly provide skill-training as well as information. As in the publishing of books, we can see a technology-driven change in the relationship between provider and client, and between the various participants in the chain of information supply and demand.

Library users are becoming much more conscious of these changes and are seeking to exploit them. In academic and special libraries – and increasingly in public libraries as well – users are aware of the potential of technology to assist in the delivery of services and information. In universities, it is now common for the library catalogue to be mounted on a network which allows academics to access the OPAC from workstations on their own desks. There is no technical reason why they should not also access databases in the same way, although where charges are involved (as they often are) this raises administrative issues which need to be addressed, and some uses of databases also raise legal questions about the copyright in the information which is retrieved. Such obstacles, however, cannot conceal the fact that the library is no longer necessarily to be defined simply as a location. It is becoming a concept. The development of the World Wide Web has significantly emphasized this trend. The Web can be browsed from any networked computer, using search engines which are designed for the non-expert user. This is yet another major shift away from the mediated, library-based, search.

As the use of computers becomes more fully integrated in the processes of teaching and learning, as well as research, the perception of the library as a building will inevitably continue to be challenged by this broader concept of information services provided through various parts of the infrastructure of a school, university or other organization. This does not mean that libraries will vanish. There will still be a need for a bookstore and perhaps for a place to study. In many cases, the library will also continue to be the most convenient location for the organization's information specialists who help employees, students and the general public to meet their information needs, even if many of the requests and replies are transmitted electronically rather than in person.

Yet even the bookstore element of the library is being challenged. All libraries have long since recognized the futility of seeking universal coverage in their own holdings of stock. For much of this century, libraries in Europe and North America have been developing relationships with one other which have allowed them and their users to share in their respective resources. The most familiar form of such cooperation is interlibrary lending, well established in the developed world for more than half a century. Different models of interlending networks have developed according to local political and financial circumstances, but the basic principle of sharing is common to all of them. Again, however, technology is enabling fundamental changes to be made in the delivery of the service. Traditionally, interlending has involved the physical movement of the desired document from the lender to the borrower. Often, the document was actually a photocopy of a journal article, to be retained by the recipient, but if originals were involved there was also a return movement. The system worked, and often worked well, yet it was both costly and time-consuming. The traditional movement of documents through interlending systems is gradually being replaced by electronic document delivery, using networks to deliver digitized data to the end-user. As the technology of digitization by scanning continues to improve, such systems will become more common.

This raises a host of complex issues which extend far beyond the traditionally perceived boundaries of librarianship. Electronic document delivery is only possible with the consent of the owners of the copyright in the original document, a restriction which does not apply to interlending, except, in a limited way, to the supply of photocopies. If we develop the scenario a little further, we have an electronic journal, available through a centralized electronic document delivery system, in which the 'library' which holds the database containing the journal is actually the 'publisher' of the journal. By this point, such words as 'library' and 'publisher' have developed so far beyond their normal meanings as to have lost them, and the boundaries between the two have all but vanished. In the academic world, this could be the most important convergence of all. As we suggested in Chapter 4, the traditional learned journal is imperilled by the cost of production and distribution; electronic equivalents can and do exist and may be the only viable way forward. If that is indeed the case, it is quite possible that the library's role will change from that of passive provider to active participant in the process of scholarly communication. Provided that the quality control mechanisms are visibly in place, there is no reason why this should not happen, nor any reason why it should be undesirable.

We must, however, be wary of overestimating the rapidity or universality of change and of assuming that it will bring universal benefits. The custodian of books and the provider of information continue to coexist, and will do so for decades to come. The mere existence of libraries, and the vast capital investment which they represent, is perhaps the most important guarantee of their future. Although there are technologies which would make it possible to digitize the world's printed books, the money to facilitate that conversion is not, and will not be, available. Moreover, there will be users whose needs will continue to be met most effectively, and perhaps some which can only be met at all, through the provision of books and documents. The majority of users of British public libraries, for example, are those borrowing books for leisure reading. For so long as that continues to be true, public libraries (which are, after all, supported by the taxes paid by their users) will continue to have to provide access to suitable book stocks. Even in academic libraries, where the demand for sophisticated information provision is greatest at the present time, scholars in many disciplines will continue to read and to publish in traditional formats because there is no practical economic alternative.

The use of new media and information technology can actually make access to information more difficult for less advantaged users, as we have suggested. It was argued in Chapter 5 that the gap between the information rich and information poor is widening as a consequence of the use of computer-based systems for information storage and the gradual elimination of traditional media for some kinds of information source and information retrieval tools. The obstacles for the information poor are many: lack of skills, equipment and the capital investment needed to provide both are only three of the most obvious. Even those with skills and access, however, can encounter serious problems. The very quantity of information which is now theoretically accessible is, paradoxically, making access to any specific piece of information more difficult. The Internet itself, one of the most potent symbols and powerful products of the information revolution, gives access to so much data that it may be doubted whether any search can realistically expect to find all the relevant information which is available through it. Indeed, the virtually unlimited capacity of users to input data which can be accessed through the Internet emphasizes how important it is for quality control mechanisms, analogous to those in traditional scholarly publishing, to be retained for those electronic communication media which may seek to emulate their traditionally published predecessors and rivals. The same considerations – the need for selectivity and for quality control – reiterate the need for information intermediaries whose skills and expertise become part of the evaluative process in transmitting information from source to user. The change is that this role is performed when the information is generated and stored, not when it is delivered to the end-user.

The use of information technology has nevertheless transformed both the library and task of the librarian, but it has done so by expansion rather than by constraint. The skills of information storage, organization, analysis and retrieval associated with librarians are now in such widespread demand that they can no longer be regarded as being uniquely associated with that single profession. At the same time, however, librarians have learned – and indeed developed – many new techniques and new skills to meet the changing demands of users and technology alike. There will be further challenges. Expert systems and knowledge-based systems, in which the computer is programmed to assist the user in finding information, have already been devised on an experimental basis to undertake some of the traditional tasks of the librarian in helping a user to search for information. These systems, which draw upon the expertise of professionals but which can then develop their own 'skills' by experience, will perhaps eventually provide the key to the efficient and well-directed use of the Internet for information retrieval purposes, for it is difficult to conceive of any mechanism not based on the use of computers which can hope to do so.

These developments have vital implications for librarians. Some of the information management skills which many of them would regard as the definition of their professional identity are becoming more widespread among those who were formerly comparatively passive consumers of the services which librarians provided. At the same time, some of the traditional skills are being displaced without alternatives being developed. The professional staff of a library – to look no further than that well-defined and 'traditional' group – increasingly find themselves dealing with the management of the institution and its systems rather than information itself. Users need advice and assistance, but much of it is at a level that can be provided by staff without traditional professional skills and qualifications. There is a real danger (if that is how it is perceived) of deprofessionalization of much of what has traditionally been associated with librarians.

At the same time, the library itself is being deinstitutionalized. Once we begin to think of a library as a concept rather than a building, it is possible to envisage, and embryonically in some places to see, an information service which is only partly dependent on the existence of a special location in which the functions of storage and use are combined. Libraries will, for reasons some of which have been suggested, continue to exist for the foreseeable future, just as it seems likely that the printed document will continue to be the most common single medium for information transfer and storage. Nevertheless, electronic or virtual 'libraries', in which information is provided by network access rather than physical contact with the information source itself, already vestigially exist. Indeed, they are the subject of much research and development work in several countries. In such a system the role of the information professional is very different from that of the familiar academic librarian. The essential function will be to devise and control systems and to manage information resources so that they are available to all legitimate network users. Professional skills are still needed, and they have something in common, at least conceptually, with the skills of the 'traditional' librarian, but those skills grow out of expertise which is based on an understanding of the management of information and information systems as well as the management of institutions and interpersonal transactions with information-seekers. Indeed, it might be argued that information professionals will be able to move back to their central professional concern with information, information systems and information media if they no longer have to manage complex institutional libraries.

Such a scenario is not the universal future for libraries and librarians. Indeed, the future is likely to be more diverse, and arguably more fragmented, than the past. Institutional libraries, in both the public sphere and in the educational world, will certainly continue to exist both as places of study and as bookstores. They will continue to provide selected materials designed to support the educational requirements and information needs, and perhaps some of the recreational demands, of their various user groups. At the same time, however, it can be expected that much teaching and learning will be delivered in other ways, dependent on computer networks, and that information support to such learning systems will itself be network based. Economic factors will force the producers and consumers of some information – such as that in scientific journals – to accept new means of access which will, in effect, circumvent the library building, while still needing some of the professional information skills which formerly made the library work. These parallel developments are neither conflicting nor incompatible. For the librarian, the challenge is to be sufficiently flexible in attitude and skills to be able to provide both. The rapid and spontaneous development of information and advice services for the general public outside rather than through existing public library systems suggests that such flexibility may not have been as widespread as might have been desirable in the recent past.

FROM ARCHIVIST TO RECORDS MANAGER

In this context, it is perhaps instructive to look at another manifestation of the information professions in the work of the archivists. Their professional skills have been challenged even more than those of librarians by the development and use of information technology. Despite apparent parallels, and some genuine similarities, librarians and archivists have always done essentially different things. The central concern of archivists is the permanent preservation of the documents in their care, but this has only been achieved at the expense of universality of coverage. Archivists are ruthless in their selection of material for preservation, to the extent that as much as 90% of the documentation created by government departments, private companies and other organizations may be deliberately destroyed so that the remaining material of long-term historical interest can be preserved, organized and made available to users.

Computers have their role in these traditional processes. Archivists, like librarians, have automated their catalogues and inventories, although perhaps not on so large a scale because of the sheer quantity of retrospective conversion that would be needed. The real impact, however, has been in the fact that computers are now both the generators and the storage systems of vast quantities of information which has traditionally been collected and preserved on paper. One obvious example is census returns. Experiments in the use of computers for storing and processing the statistical data generated by population censuses were first undertaken in the 1950s. Since the 1960s, computers have regularly been used for this purpose. The problem for the archivist is that in order to preserve the data it is also necessary either to preserve the hardware through which the data is accessible or to ensure that data is copied into new formats. This remains a constant problem as systems are now normally replaced in a time frame shorter than the intervals between the censuses themselves. Archivists were thus forced to address issues raised by electronic information systems as soon as those systems began to be used in activities which traditionally generated archival documents.

Partly because of the very different issues raised by electronic archives, not least in terms of the quantity of data generated (quite apart form the preservation of both information and media), a new and largely separate branch of the profession emerged, known as records management. The role of records managers is only partly archival. Their primary concern is to ensure that the documentation generated by an organization (whether on paper or in digitized form) is organized and stored in a retrievable way. Much of this data is ephemeral, and may be destroyed within months, or even days, of its creation. Some is of more permanent value, and some, such as employee records, or financial accounts, may even have to be preserved for legal reasons. The task of the records manager is to ensure that the various criteria for destruction and preservation are defined and met in line with the organization's obligations and wishes.

With the growth in the use of computers to meet the information needs of organizations, the role of the records manager has become more complex and more important. It is closely related to that of the systems manager, sometimes it more closely resembles the work of the manager of a management information system than that of an archivist. The records manager needs many of the skills of selection and preservation traditionally associated with the archivist, but again we can see the breaking down of traditional boundaries and the increasing difficulties of developing precise definitions of the work of information professionals and the distinctions between them. The records manager, unlike the publisher, the librarian or the archivist, generally operates on the boundaries between the public and private spheres, and perhaps more often in the latter. Publishers, librarians and archivists are all, for the most part, concerned with information which is intended for wide dissemination and public access. The records manager, like some other information professionals, is principally concerned with information collected by an organization for its own purposes and whose availability and circulation is strictly controlled. Generically, this may be described as management information, that is, information that will influence decision-making. While the decisions may be made public, the information which underlies them, at least in its raw form, generally is not.

The private information collected by governments and their agencies, and by companies, is often of immense value. This is perhaps most obviously true where it has a direct commercial relevance. Companies collect information about their markets and their rivals. Much of this may be derived from sources which are in the public domain, but its collection, processing and analysis is a long and expensive process. The value which is added by the process – to an understanding of a commercial rival's market share, for example – is the result of an investment which there is a legitimate need to protect. The management of this information, and of the systems in which it is housed, uses many of the techniques of public information work in libraries and archives, but is fundamentally different in philosophy.

INFORMATION MANAGERS

Information managers who are running management information systems, decision support systems and similar operations, whether in the public or the private sector, are essentially working for their own organizations, not providing a service to outside clients. Traditionally, these managers have not seen themselves as part of the same profession as librarians and archivists, and have only rarely come from the same educational background or training procedures. Technology, however, is creating a commonality of approach, which is probably leading to a convergence even across what has traditionally been a strongly marked boundary. It is certainly the case that in some companies the distinctions are vanishing. Where once there was a clear difference between the provision of technical information to support research and development activities (in a library), marketing information to support sales (within the sales department) and administrative information to support the management infrastructure, all three are increasingly seen as different aspects of the same problem: the provision of effective information to those who need it. The organization of the personnel through whom it is provided has become more fluid as it is recognized that many of the techniques and much of the expensive technology are common to all three strands of information management within the organization.

In Britain, these developments have perhaps been most widely publicized in the health care sector. The long-established system of universal public provision supported by taxation has been fundamentally changed in recent years for political reasons. Those changes highlighted the need for more effective information management at all levels. The underlying philosophy of the changes in health care provision was to force providers to operate in a 'market' in which they buy and sell services to one other's patients. The general practitioner with a patient who needs a particular surgical procedure can 'buy' the operation from a hospital which has the capacity to deliver it, at a price agreed between them. Although the money used for these transactions is still derived ultimately from taxation, its use was intended to simulate the use of money in the private sector.

To support the market orientation of the reorganized health service, a vast information infrastructure was created. In the early years, many serious errors were made, largely through ignorance, and there was a number of highly publicized cases of hugely expensive and ultimately useless computer systems being bought or developed by those with insufficient expertise to manage the projects for which they were responsible. There has, however, been a gradual recognition of the need to develop information management expertise in the sector, or to import it from outside. An infrastructure of training and skill development gradually evolved in the early 1990s. Information management became the linchpin upon which the whole system depended. In the general practitioner's surgery, patient records are automated. Class-ification systems have been developed which allow diseases and conditions on the one hand, and treatments on the other, to be encoded, and perhaps ultimately matched through the use of expert systems or decision support systems. Hospitals manage their waiting lists, and match patient needs with the availability of facilities and expertise, in even more complex systems. The management of the whole system of 'payments' largely depends on the effective operation of systems that record the transactions which have taken place. A sector that once employed a few score librarians as its only information professionals is now irrevocably committed to the use of information professionals at the core of the management of its activities. It has become the archetype of the management of information in the private domain.

The management of health information, however, also impin-ges, through the records of individual patients, on the most diffi-cult area of all, that of personal information. In a technical sense, there is no distinction that can usefully be made between how different kinds of information are stored. A public document (such as a library catalogue), a private record (such as the transactions between a general practice and a hospital) and personal data (such as a bank account) all use the same technology, and apply it in much the same way in the creation and maintenance of carefully designed and structured databases which allow the information to be retrieved in the desired format. The differences lie in access rather than storage. As we have seen in Chapter 6, the law regulates some aspects of this, especially in the control of access to (and to a lesser extent accuracy of) private information about identifiable individuals. Beyond the law, however, there are broadly recognized ethical requirements on information professionals about the use that they make of information that they obtain in performing their duties. Professional bodies have tried, with some success, to define these ethical constraints, but with more success in the traditional fields such as librarianship and archive work than in the new work sectors for information professionals that are appearing across the whole spectrum of government, industry and public services.

The adoption of computers as the almost universal tool of information storage and retrieval has made it difficult and perhaps futile to attempt to put a fence around the information professions. As the computer revolution continues, more and more work will be concerned with information handling, even in the manufacturing and production sectors where the processes involved are themselves increasingly automated and computer controlled and thus information dependent. Computers have made explicit what has always been implicit but hidden, ignored, and perhaps even unrecognized: that all work which involves making decisions also involves the use of information. Without information, decisions are merely guesses. As information supply becomes more efficient, more accurate and more accessible, the basis for decision-making improves. Ultimately, the quality of the decision will still depend on the interpretative skills of the decision-maker, but the information provider can at least try to ensure that those skills are deployed to the best advantage on the basis of comprehensive knowledge.

In that sense, all 'professional' work, and much that would not be traditionally identified as being professional at all, is information work. In practice, however, decision-makers are dependent on a flow of information that comes to them through intermediaries. These intermediaries may be colleagues whether as managers or subordinates, or people from outside their own organizations. Ultimately, however, the information that they provide – if it is to be accurate and useful – is drawn from verifiable and reliable sources, accessible to them, from which they can derive what they need and then package it in a form appropriate for the end-user. This intermediary role is that of the information professional, whatever the job title of the person undertaking it.

AFTERWORD

An information society?

It may seem strange at this stage to put a question mark at the end of the title of this last section. There is, however, a real question to be answered. Throughout this book, there has been an emphasis on fundamental continuities as well as profound change. The step from cuneiform to computer was a huge one, encompassing almost the whole consciously recorded history of mankind, and yet in another sense it was not so great. Our remote ancestors who recorded their activities and tried to control their systems of government were responding to the same instincts and imperatives that still drive us today. We have developed previously unimaginable technologies, and new techniques to accompany them, and perhaps we are more systematic in our approach to our use of them, but is the change really more significant than the continuity? If ours is an 'information society', was not the same true of ancient Babylon?

Implicit in the use of the phrase is the suggestion that the information society is a product of the use of computers and other electronic and audiovisual media. In this narrower sense, change has clearly been fundamental. Devices that are now part of our everyday lives – telephones, televisions, computers – were invented within the last century or so and have clearly transformed the way we live and work. That transformation has taken place within a timescale as short as a decade in many aspects of office management, telecommunications and some forms of television broadcasting. It will continue, and there is every reason to suppose that the pace of change in the immediate future will be as fast as it has been in the immediate past. Indeed, experience and historical examples would suggest that the pace will, if anything, increase.

Much of this book has been concerned with the consequences of these changes. We have traced the development and impact of a market-place in which information and the media that carry it are commodities to be traded between suppliers and consumers. We have considered some of the social and political issues that have arisen out of the existence of the market-place and the demand for information that created and sustains it. Some of these issues are new, but many are old, although they have been redefined as a consequence of technological innovation. The ownership of information has been a matter of discussion since the sixteenth century, and regulated by the law for nearly 300 years. Access to information has been a matter of concern to both governments and governed for at least as long. The cost of information, and of the provision of services through which it can be accessed, are both questions with a long ancestry. Yet the way in which these questions are now formulated, and the urgency with which they need to be answered, is indeed different. It is that difference which has a technological origin.

The computer has already been responsible for the most important change in human communications since the invention of printing, and, arguably, since the invention of writing itself. Indeed, printing was merely a development of writing, a technology which enabled writing to become more widespread and the written word to be more uniform and perhaps more reliable. Computing offers far more than that, because it gives the facility, which printing and writing never gave, for instantaneous communication on many different levels. Through the interlinking of computers and telecommunications systems – information technology – individuals can communicate with one other, can access vast stores of information, and can store information for themselves. The form, time and place of output can be largely determined by the convenience of the user rather than that of the provider. At the basis of this lies a common technology, which, while it is vastly complicated, has become so simple that all but a handful of its users can actually ignore its complications. Using a computer has become as much a part of life in the late twentieth century as switching on an electric light or driving a car.

It is in this ease and universality of access that there lies the key to the information technology revolution and the society that is developing around it. We have indeed always been dependent upon information, but we are now also dependent upon a technology that stores that information for us. In a sense that was always true, but the computer is much more than a passive store like a book or a library. When appropriately instructed, a computer can process and analyse information, and communicate it to other computers. It is this capacity for interactivity with other computers which puts their users in a uniquely powerful position, and differentiates computers themselves fundamentally from all previous mechanisms for the storage and retrieval of information. The combination of the virtually unlimited storage capacity of the computer with a processing power that is also, for all practical purposes, unlimited, makes it a unique and unprecedentedly powerful and potentially dangerous tool. If we are, as a society, concerned about such issues as data protection, it is because we are conscious of the ease with which information can be stored, sorted and retrieved. If we are concerned about the viability of our systems of scholarly communications, it is because we can see the potential of information technology to displace those that we have with something so different, perhaps so much more powerful, that we both fear it and welcome it.

In this narrower sense, the information society can perhaps best be understood as a society that has developed information technology and is learning how to use it. We are at a very early stage in this process. The computer itself is barely 50 years old even in its most primitive form. In its familiar form, as a desktop microcomputer, it has been with us for less than twenty years. The communications networks that now link millions of such machines across the globe are less than half that age. New devices and new applications are being developed every day. It is, however, clear, that the revolution is irreversible. Nothing will ever be the same again. Like nuclear energy, the power of the computer will have to be controlled if it is to work for our benefit, and we have not yet fully absorbed all its implications for the relations between individuals, the states of which they are citizens, and indeed between states themselves. At one level, the computer is an empowering tool, which gives unprecedented access to information and to communications; at another, it might be seen as an implement of control, giving unlimited power to those who control the information that it stores. The central dilemma of the information society is how to resolve that issue.

A NOTE ON FURTHER READING

L ike the book itself, this note is intended to give guidance to the novice rather than the specialist. There is a large and still growing literature on almost every aspect of the subject. Technological innovation is so rapid that few can follow it comprehensively in the specialist literature. Indeed, perhaps the best sources of information and interpretation are the newspapers; in Britain, both the *Guardian* and the *Independent* have regular, well-informed and intelligent pages on information technology issues, and the social and political dimensions are dealt with, either directly or by implication, throughout the press and the broadcast media. At a slightly more specialized level, both *New Scientist* and *Scientific American* contain a great deal of relevant material. On a more considered basis the issues are also addressed by generalist writers from Alvin Toffler to Paul Kennedy. To understand such issues, there is no real substitute for a wide awareness of current events and concerns.

More specifically, two recent books aimed at a similar audience to this one have covered some of the same ground, and can usefully be read in conjunction with it. These are: Paul F. Burton, *Information technology and society: implications for the information professions*, Library Association Publishing, 1992; and Kevin McGarry, *The changing context of information: an introductory analysis*, 2nd edn, Library Association Publishing, 1993. Both books differ in scope from one another and from this volume, but they do overlap, and provide different approaches to many topics, as well as good references and bibliographies. Inevitably, in such a rapidly changing field, monographs and textbooks are soon dated, but some have a more permanent value by raising long-term issues. Such works include R.L. Katz, *The information society: an international perspective*, Praeger, 1988; David Lyon, *The information society: issues and illusions*, Policy Press, 1987; and William J. Martin, *The information society*, Aslib, 1988. Two classic studies, of which every student should be aware, are Fritz Machlup, *The production and distribution of knowledge in the United States*, Princeton University Press, 1962; and Marc Porat, *The information economy: definition and measurement*, United States Department of Commerce, 1977.

Further study of the historical subjects in Chapters 1 and 2 can be pursued in Elizabeth Eisenstein, *The printing press as an agent of change: communications and culture in early modern Europe*, 2 vols., Cambridge University Press, 1979; and Peter Hall and Paschal Preston, *The carrier wave: new information technologies and the geography of information 1846–2003*, Unwin Hyman, 1988. More specialized historical studies abound. On technological matters, a good introduction will be found in Jack Meadows, *Info-technology: changing the way we communicate*, Cassell, 1989.

Different forms of communication systems, such as those provided by publishers, authors, librarians and educators, are dealt with in A. J. Meadows (ed.), *Knowledge and communication: essays on the information chain*, Library Association Publishing, 1991. On publishing, the best general introduction is probably Giles N. Clark, *Inside book publishing: a career builder's guide*, Blueprint, 1988, although this is a description of operations rather than a consideration of issues. On a broader canvas, the work of Philip G. Altbach, especially in *The knowledge context: comparative perspectives on the distribution of knowledge*, State University of New York Press, 1987, is seminal and cannot be ignored.

One recent study, among many, of the political issues raised here is John D. Baxter, *State security, privacy and information*, Harvester, 1990. On a more general level, see Jane Steele and Nick Moore, *Information-intensive Britain: an analysis of the policy issues,*

Policy Studies Institute, 1991; and Ian Miles, *Information technology and information society: options for the future*, Economic and Social Research Council, 1988. On the issues dealt with in Chapter 5, see Trevor Hayward, *Info-rich, Info-poor: access and exchange in the global information society*, Bowker-Saur, 1995; and Mohan Munasinghe (ed.), *Computers and informatics in developing countries*, Butterworth, 1989.

The literature teems with speculative studies on the future of the information professions. This cannot be disentangled from the future of the services they provide, so that many insights can be found in such documents as *New library: the people's network* < URL:http://www.ukoln.ac.uk/services/lic.newlibrary/ > , Chapter 3.

INDEX